A WORLD
GONE MAD

1 sept. 1939

6" I dag började kriget.
Ingen ville tro det.
I går eftermiddag satt
Elsa Gullander o. jag i
Vasaparken och barnen
sprang och lekte runt
omkring oss och vi
skällde i all gemyt-
lighet på Hitler och
kom överens om att
det nog *inte* skulle
bli krig — och
idag! Tyskarna
har bombarderat
flera polska städer
tidigt i morse,
och trängt in i
Polen på i alla håll.
Jag har i det

A WORLD GONE MAD

The Diaries of
Astrid Lindgren 1939–45

Astrid Lindgren

Translated from the Swedish
by Sarah Death

With a foreword by Karin Nyman

PUSHKIN PRESS
LONDON

Pushkin Press
71–75 Shelton Street, London WC2H 9JQ

Original text © Astrid Lindgren / Saltkråkan AB 2015

Foreword by Karin Nyman

Reproduction of the diaries © Andrea Davis Kronlund,
The National Library of Sweden, Stockholm

English translation © Sarah Death, 2016

The photograph on page 6 is by Ricard Estay.
All other photographs are courtesy of Saltkråkan AB.

A World Gone Mad first published by Salikon Förlag, Sweden, 2015,
under the title Krigsdagböcker 1939–1945.

For more information about Astrid Lindgren, see
www.astridlindgren.com.

The translation was supported by a grant
from the Swedish Arts Council

First published in Great Britain by Pushkin Press in 2016

ISBN 978 1 782272 31 1

1 3 5 7 9 8 6 4 2

Set in Monotype Dante by Tetragon, London
Printed and bound by CPI Group (UK) Ltd, Croydon CRO 4YY

www.pushkinpress.com

Contents

Foreword
by Karin Nyman

I was five at the outbreak of the Second World War. For us children in Sweden it soon started to feel like a normal state of affairs, almost a natural state, for all those around us to be at war. We took it for granted that our country had somehow secured guarantees not to be involved, and it was constantly being stressed to us: No, no, don't be scared, the war won't be coming to *Sweden*. It felt special, but in some strange way reasonable and justified, for us to be the ones who were spared.

It did not seem strange to me that my mother cut articles out of the papers and pasted them into exercise books; I assumed it was just something parents did. Now I know that she was very probably unique, a 32-year-old housewife with secretarial training but no experience of thinking in political terms, who was so determined to document what was happening in Europe and the world to her own satisfaction that she persisted with her cuttings and commentaries for all six years of the war. It is also extremely rare and special to find diary entries so well written that they can be reproduced unabridged and instantly make gripping reading.

That is why Salikon Förlag originally wanted to publish them, of course, because they give such a good picture of ordinary family life in Sweden in the war years and so vividly express the despair of the powerless at the horrors they read about in the papers every morning. Daily papers were the primary news source, there was no television, and although there was radio it had no live broadcasting or correspondents – the radio news consisted of readings of the telegrams received from the Swedish news agency Tidningarnas Telegrambyrå (TT).

After the first year of the war, however, Astrid gained access to a fresh source of information. She was offered state security work at the secret Postal Control Division, as a censor of military and private post sent to, and coming from, other counties. The letters had to be steamed open and read, the aim being to find and black out any locations of military importance or other classified information. It was all so hush-hush that we children never knew what her late-evening job was. But the restrictions did not prevent her from copying out, or quoting sections of, the more interesting letters in her diary, for the insight they gave into conditions in the occupied countries.

The diaries show another side of Astrid Lindgren's authorship. She was admittedly still not a published author, nor had she any intention of becoming one. But in the midst of the convulsive tensions of the time, at some point in the winter of 1941, she started coming out with her unbridled stories of wild, freedom-loving Pippi Longstocking – first as a bedtime story for me, then at any time of day, for a growing audience of children, her own and others', all wanting to hear more. In early 1944, she wrote down some of the stories and made them into a book. It was published by Rabén & Sjögrens Förlag in 1945, having first being refused by Bonniers. That was how it all began. It rather takes your breath away to think that before that relatively recent date, Pippi Longstocking simply did not exist and Astrid Lindgren could not have had the faintest idea of the career as a children's writer which lay ahead of her.

And that she, and we, did not know was probably just as well! How utterly unreal a glimpse of her future global fame would have seemed to her then. I can imagine that she might have looked away in terror at the sight of it. In old age, with her renown a fait accompli and her eyesight too poor for her to read the piles of readers' thank-you letters and their touching testaments to the crucial role some of her books had played in their lives, when I had to read the letters out loud to her, she would sometimes look up, interrupt me and say, sounding almost fearful: 'But this is remarkable, don't you think?' 'Well yes,' I would say, because I did. Truly remarkable.

Translator's Note

Until 2013, seventeen leather-bound diaries lived in a wicker laundry basket at Astrid Lindgren's familiar home address, 46 Dalagatan in Stockholm. The diaries cover the years 1939–45. Her own name for them was 'The War Diaries' and they are now accessible to the public for the first time. The diaries bulged with press cuttings, pasted in between Lindgren's handwritten entries. She refers now and then to the time it has taken her to save newspapers and magazines, sift through them and select items to cut out for pasting into her note-books, but it was a task she set herself and she carried it through to the end, the number of cuttings increasing with every passing wartime year. In her preface to the Swedish edition, Kerstin Ekman, another eminent Swedish writer, expresses her admiration for Lindgren's unusual resolve:

> War diaries were kept by general staffs and units out in the field. Their operational maps, battle accounts and observations would form the foundation of future history writing. It is striking to think of this 32-year-old mother of two and office-worker taking on the same sort of task with such seriousness. But only for herself, to try to understand what was going on.

The Swedish edition includes facsimiles of quite a number of the two-page diary spreads featuring pasted-in newspaper cuttings. Here and there in this edition the reader will come across references to such accompanying cuttings and Pushkin Press has asked me to provide an explanatory note wherever one is necessary.

Astrid Lindgren's own comments are in round brackets, whereas square brackets indicate clarifications added by the Swedish editors, with a few additions for this English-language edition, to provide a little more background information for a non-Swedish readership.

The ambition was to retain the overall character of the original, but dates and abbreviations have been harmonized. Biographical names have been corrected and some place names have been put into English. Where the original work was in English, or in long lists of Swedish works, book and film titles have also been rendered in English.

Then as now, Swedes often use 'England' as shorthand for any part of the British Isles, and that is Lindgren's practice throughout her diaries. It seemed less jarring to render this as 'Britain' in the English-language edition.

SARAH DEATH

1939

Astrid and her husband Sture at home in Vulcanusgatan, 1939.

Oh! War broke out today. Nobody could believe it.

Yesterday afternoon, Elsa Gullander and I were in Vasa Park with the children running and playing around us and we sat there giving Hitler a nice, cosy telling-off and agreed that there definitely was *not* going to be a war – and now today! The Germans bombarded several Polish cities early this morning and are forging their way into Poland from all directions. I've managed to restrain myself from any hoarding until now, but today I laid in a little cocoa, a little tea, a small amount of soap and a few other things.

A terrible despondency weighs on everything and everyone. The radio churns out news reports all day long. Lots of our men are being called up. There's a ban on private motoring, too. God help our poor planet in the grip of this madness!

2 SEPTEMBER

A sad, sad day! I read the war announcements and felt sure Sture would be called up but he turned out not to be, in the end. Countless others have got to leave home and report for duty, though. We're in a state of 'intensified war readiness'. The amount of stockpiling is unbelievable, according to the papers. People are mainly buying coffee, toilet soap, household cleaning soap and spices. There's apparently enough sugar in the country to last us 15 months, but if nobody can resist stocking up we'll have a shortage anyway. At the grocer's there wasn't a single kilo of sugar to be had (but they're expecting more in, of course).

When I went to my coffee merchant to buy a fully legitimate quarter-kilo of coffee, I found a notice on the door: 'Closed. Sold out for today.'

It's Children's Day today, and dear me, what a day for it! I took Karin up to the park this afternoon and that was when I saw the official notice that all men born in 1898 [Sture's year of birth] would be called up. I tried to read the newspaper while Karin went on the slide but I couldn't, I just sat there with tears rising in my throat.

People look pretty much as usual, only a bit more gloomy. Everybody talks about the war all the time, even people who don't know each other.

3 SEPTEMBER

The sun is shining, it's a nice warm day, this earth could be a lovely place to live. At 11 a.m. today Britain declared war on Germany, as did France, but I don't know exactly what time. Germany had received an ultimatum from Britain demanding an undertaking by 11 o'clock to withdraw its troops from Poland and enter into talks, in which case the invasion of Poland would be deemed never to have happened. But no undertaking had been received by 11 o'clock and Chamberlain said in his speech to the British nation on this Sunday afternoon: 'consequently this country is at war with Germany'.

'Responsibility [...] lies on the shoulders of one man,' Chamberlain told the British parliament. And history's judgment of Hitler will certainly be damning – if this turns into another world war. Many people see this quite simply as the fall of the white race and of civilization.

The various governments are already jawing about who's to blame. Germany claims that Poland attacked first and that the Poles could do whatever they wanted under the protection of the Anglo-French guarantee. Here in Sweden we can't see it any other way than that Hitler *wants* war, or that he can't see any means to avoid it without losing face. It's pretty clear that Chamberlain did his utmost to keep the peace; he gave way in Munich for no other reason. This time, Hitler demanded 'Danzig and the Corridor' but deep down he probably wants to rule the whole world. What line should Italy and Russia take? Polish sources say the first two days of war cost 1,500 lives in Poland.

4 SEPTEMBER

Anne-Marie came round this evening and we have never had a more dismal 'meeting'. We *tried* to talk about things other than the war, but it was impossible. In the end we had a brandy to cheer ourselves up, but it didn't help.

A big British passenger steamer with 1,400 people on board has been torpedoed by the Germans, who *deny* having done it and claim the ship must have run into a mine. But the British wouldn't have laid mines off the north-west coast of Scotland. I believe all the surviving passengers were rescued (60 died, no, more, 128?), some of them by Wenner-Gren on the *Southern Cross*, out on a pleasure trip with his tanks full of the oil he's been hoarding. He's been scolded roundly in the press for his crazy stockpiling.

The British mounted a bombing raid over Germany and dropped not bombs but leaflets – saying that the British people don't want to be at war with the German people, only with the Nazi regime. The

British presumably hope there'll be a revolution in Germany. It'll annoy Hitler, at any rate. He's decreed hard labour for anyone caught listening to foreign radio stations and the death penalty for those spreading information from foreign broadcasts to other citizens.

A bomb from an unidentified plane fell on Esbjerg in peaceable little Denmark, destroyed a house and killed two people, one of them a woman.

The bus service in Stockholm is to be restricted from tomorrow. Our streets already look deserted, now that use of private cars has been banned.

Today I assembled my little stockpile in a corner of the kitchen, ready for storage in the attic. It comprises: 2kg sugar, 1kg sugar lumps, 3kg rice, 1kg potato flour, 1½kg coffee in various tins, 2kg household cleaning soap, 2 boxes Persil, 3 bars toilet soap, 5 packets cocoa, 4 packets tea and a few spices. I shall gradually try to collect up a bit more, because prices are bound to rise soon. Karin called for a drink of water after I put her to bed last night. 'At least we don't have to worry about saving water.' She thought we'd be able to live on water and jam if we had a war.

5 SEPTEMBER

Chamberlain delivered a radio address to the German people – who aren't allowed to listen.

There's still nothing happening on the western front. But it seems clear that Germany is giving Poland a good thrashing.

I bought shoes for myself and the kids, before the prices go up: two pairs for Karin at 12.50 kronor a pair, one pair for Lasse at 19.50 and one pair for me at 22.50.

6 SEPTEMBER

They say the French put up placards on the western front: 'We won't shoot.' And that the Germans replied on their placards: 'Nor will we!' But it can't be true.

From tomorrow, all heavy goods vehicles will be subject to restrictions, as well.

7 SEPTEMBER

All quiet at the Schipka Pass [on the Swedish island of Gotska Sandön, strategically placed in the Baltic]. But the Germans will soon be in Warsaw.

8 SEPTEMBER

Yes, they've made it. Poor Poland! The Poles maintain that if the Germans were able to take Warsaw, it means the last Polish soldier has been crushed.

17 SEPTEMBER

The Russians marched into Poland today as well, 'to safeguard the interests of the Russian minority'. Poland's now as far down on its knees as it can get, so they must be thinking of sending a negotiator to Germany.

There's still not much action on the western front, but according to today's paper Hitler's planning a huge air offensive against Britain. We hear of very worrying developments at sea: countless ships torpedoed or blown up by mines. Supply routes to Germany must be more or less cut off, I think.

3 OCTOBER

The war carries on as usual. Poland has surrendered. It's total chaos there. Germany and Russia have divided the country between them. It seems simply incredible that such a thing can happen in the twentieth century.

Russia is the one benefiting most from this war. Once the Germans had crushed Poland – only then did the Russians march in and take their share of the spoils, and no small share, either. It's generally assumed that the Germans aren't particularly happy about this state of affairs, but they can't say anything. Russia's making a whole series of demands in the Baltic states – and getting what it wants.

There can be no doubt that Germany is waging war on us, the neutral countries. All our ships in the North Sea are being captured and sunk. They've got spies in the ports checking up on cargoes and destinations, and we're not the only neutral country whose ships are being sunk. I can't see what they hope to achieve.

There's still nothing much happening on the western front.

Here at home, we have various minor inconveniences to cope with. There's no white sewing thread to be had, for instance. And we're only allowed a quarter-kilo of household soap at a time.

Lots of people are now unemployed as a result of the crisis. It's a shame nobody's shot Hitler. The coming week is going to be 'dramatic', Germany and Britain have both promised. Germany's expected to propose a peace treaty that Britain can't accept. But people all over the world want peace.

14 OCTOBER

The punch-up has started in earnest and it affects us now, primarily Finland of course, but it's only a short step from there to here. Russia's 'invited' the foreign ministers of the Baltic states to Moscow, one by one, and now it's Finland's turn. Foreign Minister Paasikivi is spending several days with Stalin, keeping Finland, us and the whole world in suspense. Helsinki has evacuated large sections of its population and the country is preparing for a war it would dearly have loved to avoid. The solidarity of the Nordic peoples is greater than ever. King Gustaf has invited all the Nordic heads of state to a conference in Stockholm next week. For now, Finland is putting its trust in Sweden. We're expecting general mobilization here soon. Lars has come home from school with a list of kit he'll need if they are evacuated and Mrs Stäckig and I went to PUB [department store] today to buy rucksacks and underwear for our lads.

A British battleship, the *Royal Oak*, has been sunk. There were 1,000 men on board; I don't know how many they were able to save.

18 OCTOBER

Today, the four Nordic heads of state and their foreign ministers gathered here in Stockholm at the invitation of King Gustaf. This historic day was favoured with brilliant sunshine and it looked very festive with all the flags flying, down in the centre of town. Pelle Dieden and I had lunch at the Opera Grill. In the evening, hundreds of thousands gathered in the area round the palace. We were at home and heard it on the radio. Around 10, their three majesties and President Kallio came out onto a balcony above Lejonbacken [the slope up to the palace] to a jubilant reception from the crowd. 'Kallio, Kallio,' they roared, so the sweet little man was forced to come out a second time. The eyes of the world are on Stockholm at the moment. Roosevelt and all the presidents of the South American republics have sent telegrams of sympathy to King Gustaf.

Paasikivi goes back to Moscow on Saturday evening and then we'll see what happens.

Paasikivi and the other Finns are still in Moscow, where they've been taking part in the festivities to commemorate the Revolution. Sillanpää has won the Nobel Prize and all the other Nordic countries are collecting money for Finland.

Nobody knows yet how things will turn out, but in the past few days the eyes of the world have been turned elsewhere. There was a bomb in Munich the other day, an assassination attempt on Hitler, who was there for the anniversary of the attempted Putsch in 1923. He made a speech in the Bürgerbräukeller, and 20 minutes after he left the hall some kind of bomb or infernal machine went off, killing 8 people and injuring 60. Unfortunately the timer was running 20 minutes slow. Though perhaps one shouldn't say unfortunately, because the attack is only generating more hate and the Germans are blaming the British for it, as they do everything else.

There's still nothing happening on the western front but the suspense is awful and everyone expects a German offensive to dwarf anything the world has ever seen.

Wilhelmina of Holland and Leopold of Belgium launched a renewed drive for peace; they treasure their poor countries.

Parts of Holland have already been deliberately flooded for defence purposes. They expect a German invasion any day.

Just imagine if we could have peace! Peace on earth! It was Armistice Day yesterday, 21 years since the end of hostilities.

30 NOVEMBER

Eli, Eli, lemi sabachtani! Who'd want to live in this world! Today the Russians bombarded Helsinki and several other places in Finland. Meanwhile they're also trying to push forward on the Karelian Isthmus, but seem to have been beaten back there. We've been poised between hope and despair for a long time, but when the Finnish delegation came home from Moscow without having reached any agreement, everything was suddenly quiet and calm. Many of those evacuated from Helsinki came back again. Then the Russians suddenly turn round and say Finnish snipers have been active on the border, which the Finns deny. But the Russians want a fight – and now they've started one, even though they have world opinion against them.

I can't remember a day as black as this! I was at the National Association of Wholesalers today. In the morning the messenger boy came in and announced the dreadful news, which none of us ever thought would really come to pass. My knees felt shaky all day; and this evening I was at Anne-Marie and Stellan's – in mourning. What lies ahead, what fate awaits us? And poor Finland!

7 DECEMBER

What terrible times we live in! Finland is keeping Russia blocked with incomparable gusto. But in their rancour, the Russians resorted to using gas yesterday. Bitter battles are raging on the Karelian Isthmus and round

Petsamo. There's been no aerial bombardment, though, because of the weather. The Russians are poorly equipped and find the snowstorms hard going. They've lost a lot of people and the whole world is full of admiration for the Finnish armed forces. But the civilian population up north, fleeing across the Swedish border, is in dire straits. Here in Sweden, people are mad keen to donate all they can to Finland. Tons of clothes and money are being collected and sent off. I went up to the attic myself the day before yesterday and grabbed up everything I could find, including Sture's 'coachman's coat' and Mother's [her mother-in-law's] gruesome cardigan. Though I think the Finns already have enough trials – without Mother's cardigan.

The whole world is intensely pro-Finland. Germany alone is holding its tongue. But Italy, its 'axis brother', is more furious with the Soviets than anyone else. The other day, 21 Italian planes landed at Bromma Airport and then flew on to Finland – though the newspapers aren't allowed to say so. Britain and America will also supply arms, on credit. America proposes cancelling Finland's war debt. But Finland expects more, of course: it wants the world to come together and do something more positive. And our newspapers are publishing appeals for us to be part of it, though they don't say so directly. Lots of Swedes are keen to go as volunteers.

Following a directive from Moscow, a Finnish Communist, a little scoundrel called Kuusinen, has set up something called the Finnish Democractic Republic in Terijoki. Finland has appealed to the League of Nations but Molotov refuses to take part in any sort of conference. Russia isn't at war with Finland, the dear little man insists, they're simply liberating the Finnish people, who are being pig-headed and refusing to let themselves be liberated.

And besides that, there's everything else to worry about; in the office today I heard rumours of general mobilization, though they probably aren't true. But Norrland has mobilized, at any rate; loads of people have been sent up there in the past few days.

On the western front there's still a ceasefire. Among the many rumours circulating there's one that says Hitler's confined to a padded cell, Göring's a broken man and power is in the hands of Goebbels, Himmler and Ribbentrop.

Today's story runs as follows:

Two earnest gentlemen on a tram.

'What is it actually about, this world war? What are they trying to achieve?'

'My dear fellow, they made that very plain before they started. It's all a matter of who is to control Danzig.'

Yes, really – that was what all this madness sprang from. But Petsamo is a long way from Danzig! And Germany will have to bear the blame in perpetuity for letting the Russian barbarians loose on Europe.

13 DECEMBER

We got a new government today. Sandler, Engberg, Strindlund and a few others have gone – though they're all as dodgy as each other if you ask me, and all just toeing the party line. But it *was* good to get rid of Sandler.

Word has it that a unit of 5,000 men set off from Sweden today to help Finland. I do hope it's true. Yesterday I was so down that I sought refuge in the word of God, and the Bible gave me the following answer: 'O Lord, there is none like thee to help, between the mighty and the weak' [II Chronicles 14:11].

If only that were true! Finland is getting by pretty well so far, but how long will that last? The League of Nations has met, but the results are meagre.

NEW YEAR'S NIGHT

The Finns have pulled off their greatest victory to date, we heard on the 7 o'clock news. They've wiped out around 1,000 Russians and captured weapons of all kinds.

But as the New Year dawns, we're left contemplating the future with dread. Will Sweden stay out or go in? There are loads of volunteers setting off for Finland. And if we do go in, presumably we'll have a theatre of war in Skåne, Germany against Britain. So people say.

At any rate, we've collected over 5 million kronor for Finland and sent loads of weapons and anti-aircraft equipment and all sorts of things.

1940

Astrid with her children Lars and Karin outside
their block of flats in Vulcanusgatan, around 1940.

As the New Year bells rang in 1940, some of our northern poets read their work on the radio. All the Nordic countries were represented, but I decided to paste in Jarl Hemmer's and Silfverstolpe's, which moved me most. Because moving was the word for it. It wasn't easy to experience the beginning of a new year. The future looks so hopeless, so menacing. Nobody can feel glad.

[Cuttings from Svenska Dagbladet, *1940:*
poems by Hemmer and Silfverstolpe]

'May You, O turner of the world, when next a new year dawns,
let us stand tall as now, in staunch resistance of lies and hate.'
[Jarl Hemmer]

15 JANUARY

Terrible bombing raids have been unleashed on poor Finland. And yet – after a month and a half of war, the Russians have won nothing, and sacrificed so many troops and materials. The other day, *Dagens Nyheter* claimed the Russians had lost 100,000 men since the start of field warfare. The intense cold has contributed to the Russians' huge losses, of course. What's more, the Finns have won a couple of major victories at Suomussalmi since the start of the New Year.

There are Swedish volunteers going off to Finland every day. And doctors. And two ambulances, thanks to Red Cross collections. The national appeal will soon have raised 9 million kronor. The saying goes that the Swedish state has chipped in with about 70 million, too. We're sending bottled blood, horse blankets, clothes and all kinds of things. We're sending neck guards and knee guards and God knows what. But still – are we doing as much as we should? Posterity will no doubt be the judge of that.

I FEBRUARY

Yesterday evening I saw Gunnar, just back from Finland, where he's been with a Farmers' Union delegation.

He was impressed by the Finnish civilians, who are carrying on as normal despite the bombs the Russians are hailing down on them. Gunnar says the planes are firing at men, women and children with machine guns. He told me about one case in which some planes went for a nursemaid and two young children. They shot and killed the nursemaid, but the children were all right, amazingly enough. There's just no sense in waging war that way, and it must be incredibly uneconomic for the Russians, too.

I've finally got a figure for the Swedish volunteers – 8,000. I hoped and believed it would be more than that. The Finns are terribly grateful to Sweden, even so. They need more people, though. Not vast numbers, but a couple of divisions would do it, they say. Because the Russians simply can't make use of all their people – and neither the men nor the materials are made of the right stuff.

Gunnar described the course of events when the Finns wiped out 12,000 Russians on the ice of Lake Kiantajärvi. The Russians came in along a road that ended in the middle of nowhere, and had to go out onto the frozen lake. Then the Finns surrounded them. Three times the Finns urged the Russians to surrender, but they have orders not to let themselves be taken alive. After the third request, the Finnish artillery and planes opened fire on the frantic troops on the ice. When 900 out of the 12,000 were left alive on the ice they surrendered, poor devils. But there are still more than 11,000 Russians lying on the Kiantajärvi ice. What will happen in the spring, when it gets warmer?

9 FEBRUARY

What a world, what an existence! Reading the papers is a depressing pastime. Bombs and machine guns hounding women and children in Finland, the oceans full of mines and submarines, neutral sailors dying, or at best being rescued in the nick of time after days and nights of privation on some wretched raft, the behind-the-scenes tragedy of the Polish population (nobody's supposed to know what's happening, but some things get into the papers anyway), special sections on the trams for 'the German master race', the Poles not allowed out after 8 in the evening, and so on. The Germans talk about their 'harsh but just treatment' of the Poles – so then we know. What hatred it will generate! In the end the world will be so full of hate that it chokes us.

I think it's God's punishment being visited on the world. And to crown it all, we are having a winter more bitter than any we can remember. Ice has made communications by sea even more difficult and there's a serious coal shortage. It's awfully cold in our flat, but we're getting used to it. We've almost abandoned the idea of fresh air and airing the place out, though we used to sleep with the window open all year round. The fuel situation in Denmark is even worse than here, and their houses aren't as well built, either. Meanwhile, I've bought a fur coat – even though doomsday is likely to arrive before I've had time to wear it out.

18 FEBRUARY

'I want to stay neutral until I die,' said Frida [the eponymous protagonist of a 1922 collection of song lyrics by the poet Birger Sjöberg] and Per Albin Hansson says the same. Some sort of indiscretion led to it leaking out to the press (*Folkets Dagblad*) that the Finnish government has asked for direct military assistance from Sweden and been refused. Per Albin was forced to provide an explanation – and it was worse than lousy. Basically he just referred back to his statement in the budget debate a month or so ago, in other words the fact that Sweden 'wants to remain neutral until its death'. God, it's terrible having to agonize like this and still not *know* which is the right line to take. The Finns, and many Swedes, think that from Sweden's point of view the wisest move would be to take up arms at once, because it's idiotic to believe that Russia, once it has crushed Finland, will simply stop at the Torne River. But the Swedish government, which ought to be in possession of all the information, doesn't want to declare open war on Russia and risk Germany turning on Sweden and making Sweden the battlefield of the two great powers. Blast Germany, if only we could be left in peace to help the Finns against the Russians. These past few days, things have been looking critical on the Mannerheim Line. The intensity of the offensive there must surely be unparalleled in world history. The Finns have retreated a bit – and Mannerheim insists the Mannerheim Line cannot be broken through – God grant that it's true!

Today, the German supply ship *Altmark* was captured by British destroyers in Norwegian territorial waters. Five hundred British prisoners were set free. And poor Norway protested in vain. Everything Germany says is couched in language full of hate, which makes one fear the worst, and Britain isn't even going to apologize to Norway for the violation of its neutrality. The impact of the sea war is still being felt mainly by the merchant navies of the neutral countries – no, I certainly want to stay neutral until I die.

They've imposed a blackout in the city for the time being and it's a thousand times more horrible than last time, because then nobody thought it could ever possibly be put to a serious test.

12 MARCH

Perhaps this is the very day when they're deciding in Moscow whether there will be peace. Through Swedish mediation, a peace conference has taken place, even though the war is raging on. Ryti, Paasikivi and two others are there. Nobody knows anything yet about the terms on which Russia will make peace, and after all, Finland isn't in a position that obliges her to agree to unreasonable demands. In actual fact, any terms are 'unreasonable', because why should Russia get a single scrap of Finland's soil?

The Western powers don't want peace between Russia and Finland at all. They like the idea of Russia being kept busy, so it can't deliver anything to Germany. They are offering Finland all the help the country wants – but first they have to receive a request for help, and there hasn't been one. This direct request has to come first, otherwise they can't just march straight through Norway and Sweden. And that's what they'd most like to do! So Sweden has been roundly scolded, particularly in the

French press, which claims we have put pressure on Finland to persuade it to make peace. The Swedish government vehemently denies this; we only conveyed the peace offer from Russia. The Western powers think Germany has made us try to broker peace. But in fact Germany has probably been on at Russia to persuade them to make peace. Because a peace agreement seems to suit Germany too darned well and the Western powers too darned badly.

A little Finnish boy was supposed to come to us by plane from Åbo [Turku] today, but we've heard nothing. Maybe he'll come tonight.

We've been entirely without hot water for over a week now.

Oh, if only there could be peace. If only Finland could have peace, at least, and we could help them rebuild their ravaged land.

I heard the news just now. No confirmed reports are available yet on the outcome of the negotiations. We'll hear at 11 o'clock this evening, if any new reports have come in. God, let there be peace. A good peace, one that Finland can accept and at least keep its right of self-determination. Let there be peace!

PEACE?!?

13 MARCH

Yes, they made peace last night! When I woke up, Sture came in with the paper, with its big headline FINLAND–SOVIET UNION PEACE. But nobody's exactly happy today. I was, a little bit, to start with, but it soon faded. This is a bitter peace. The Russians are to get Hangö [Hanko] for 30 years and set up a naval base there. The Karelian Isthmus, with Vyborg [Viipuri] and the western bank of Lake Ladoga plus Sortavala, are to be ceded to Russia. Hostilities ceased at noon today. It's a relief to know that no more women and children will be murdered, of course, but it's still a bitter pill to swallow. Bitterest of all is the fact that the Finnish government asked Sweden to let British and French troops through, but was refused. I expect there'll be great animosity towards us, out there in the world. And yet – if we'd agreed, it would have been tantamount to unleashing war between the great powers on our territory. But right now, Germany is triumphant.

Rauno Virtanen was here today. He came by plane from Åbo [Turku] last night. Seeing him sit there, fighting back his tears, was one of the worst things I've experienced for a long time.

13 March 1940 has been a hard day.

9 APRIL

Peace – wasn't it? No, no – as far from peace as ever! I'm so deathly tired this evening that I can hardly write.

Since early this morning, Norway has been at war with Germany. Denmark has been occupied by the Germans, who took over the entire Danish administration and met no resistance. Telephone links to Norway have been cut, but the Norwegians seem to be putting up a fight, for the time being. Germany's reason for taking over 'the armed protection of Norwegian neutrality' is officially that, yesterday or the day before, the British mined Norwegian waters to stop the transport of iron ore from Narvik to Germany. But the German assault has no doubt been planned for a long time. Troops have landed here, there and everywhere. Bergen, Trondheim, Oslo and various other places are occupied. The Norwegian government has taken itself off to Hamar. The Allies have pledged Norway immediate help.

So now the Nordic countries are a theatre of war after all, and Sweden is the only one of them not to have experienced foreign troops on its soil. *The peaceful corner of Europe* [in English], ha ha! We're braced for general mobilization and it's probably only a matter of time before the Germans decide to 'defend' our neutrality, too.

I was at Rudling's solicitor's office today when I heard the dreadful news. Rudling came in and said in his usual, quiet way: 'Well – it's war, so I don't know if there's much point carrying on with this.' I felt the blood rushing through my body. My first thought was to dash home to the children, but in the end I stayed there, writing letters about divorce and the law on sale of movable property. Out on the streets, people look the same as usual. I suppose we're getting used to it now.

But I'm so fed up that the chance to be happy has been snatched away. Just when it's finally over in Finland and we ought to be happy that the sun's shining again after the terrible winter and look forward to spring and summer, along comes a new blow, more crushing than ever. We're back to not daring to look even a day ahead. We can't plan anything. All we can plan for is evacuation. And I provided the required details this evening.

12 APRIL

12 April 1940 – it was a day of alarm, anxiety and distress in Stockholm. The air is abuzz with rumours – word was that at 6 o'clock today, Germany would be informed whether we'd allow its troops to march through to Norway, but it could just be a rumour like all the rest. Everybody's talking, everybody's heard different rumours, everybody wants to get out of town. Sture received a special-delivery letter at noon today about reporting for military duty and at 3.15 he went off on the bus to Spånga. I haven't heard anything from him. In practice this is general mobilization, even though they're not calling it that.

They say some of the schools have closed. I wish Norra Latin would close, too, because then I'd take the children straight home to Näs [where she grew up, in the Småland countryside]. Unfortunately Karin's in bed with a temperature and a sore throat, which feels appropriate somehow, with everything else being so rotten.

It feels rather desolate, being left with sole responsibility for the children in times like these. Anne-Marie is leaving with her three tomorrow. I expect it's the thought of Oslo being caught napping that's made people here want to get out. If only we knew what was coming!

13 APRIL

69 2-1918 Lindgren of the veteran reserve came home on his first leave. 'Never will the memory fade, of how splendid he appeared,' [a line of verse from Johan Ludvig Runeberg's *The Tales of Ensign Stål*]. A tiny little peaked cap on the crown of his head and a gloriously ugly, ill-fitting uniform coat. Under that a short jacket and a thick sweater, with trousers that are way too tight and pull across the stomach. The whole family gathered round him and laughed. But there's not much else to laugh about. He hasn't had a bite to eat since lunch here yesterday, when his marching orders arrived. He couldn't face eating out of greasy mess tins. He tucked into his roast meat and potatoes with a hearty appetite. He'd spent the night fully clothed and wrapped in his civilian overcoat, lying on the floor with just a bit of straw for padding. He froze to the bone. We lent him Lasse's sleeping bag and pillowcase, and some cutlery, to help him cope with the worst of it. At 10 o'clock he had to venture out into the foul weather and go back to Spånga. I couldn't help feeling sorry for him.

What an awfully dismal day! Grey, grey, with persistent sleet. Karin still in bed. Lars out with the Scouts. And Sture rang to say he couldn't get a leave of absence.

Then Stellan came round and a bit later Sture turned up after all. He had to go back at half-past eight, though. After that, Alli, Elsa, Karin L. [Litiäinen]. and I went to the pictures. *Juninatten* [*June Night*, starring Ingrid Bergman]. But it's hopeless trying to relax. The nightmare hangs over you all the time. The British have mined the whole Baltic Sea, except for Swedish territorial waters. In Norway, the war continues unabated. King Haakon is being targeted by bombers and had to take to the forest. It was largely as a result of treachery that Germany's surprise attack on Norway succeeded. The Norwegian Nazis have betrayed their country. But resistance is going well in the far north, at any rate, and the British and Norwegians have apparently retaken Narvik.

A look into the future offers a pretty gloomy prospect, even if we're lucky enough to avoid the war. Our exports to the West have seized up entirely. And our imports, of course. The gas board's warning us that the situation could get critical if we don't cut down on gas consumption, but goodness knows how we're supposed to cut down when we need the gas for heating water. Before long we could find ourselves without any gas at all, and then what? Gas-meter tokens have gone up from 20 to 25 öre and a single on the tram costs 20 öre now. Electric power is dearer, food is dearer, sugar went up again the other day by four öre a kg and is now rationed, like tea and coffee. But I'm sure this is just the beginning for us; the total blockade hasn't been in force for long. So we can always comfort ourselves with the thought that it'll only get worse.

In Norway, the punch-up continues. So many towns and villages have been devastated by the bombing. So many people are homeless. I think it must be worse living in Norway than it was in Finland, because the internal front in Norway has let it down so woefully. Norwegian resistance overall seems to have been pretty lame. The Allies' contribution so far has been less than useless. Though they are apparently there in considerable force, both the British and the Germans. In the far north the Norwegian mobilization went more or less to plan and the British are in control of the situation up there. But all of southern Norway is in German hands and they're advancing with terrible intensity and efficiency. There was a big press conference in Berlin where Ribbentrop gave a speech and produced documents proving that the Allies had plans to invade Norway, which were only foiled by Germany intervention. They also made claims that the Norwegian government hasn't been absolutely neutral. On the other hand, Ribbentrop said that the Swedish government had observed strict neutrality. The foreign press is saying Sweden's position has improved considerably. But we're still on a state of high military alert, and we hope that won't change until this wretched war finally ends.

Spring is here! 'O, hur härligt majsol ler' ['How the glorious May sun smiles'], the Uppsala students sang [in their traditional serenade to the spring] on the radio on Walpurgis Night, and it was almost unbearably lovely to hear. We had sparkling sunshine all through the public holiday and it's finally a bit warmer after that awful winter. Yesterday virtually the whole of Stockholm marched in procession to Gärdet for a unified, cross-party demonstration. Mrs Stäckig and Göran were there with me and the children, watching. The whole city was a hive of activity.

Today, Karin and I were out at [the woods and lake at] Judarn and could really see that spring had arrived. There's something so odd about the spring this year: one can't help being cheered up by it but at the same time it feels even more unbearable to think of people killing each other with the sun shining and the flowers budding.

6 MAY

Some days ago, the British got back on board their ships and gave up Norway, or at any rate all of it except for Narvik. So that leaves the Norwegians without any allies. The entire south of Norway is German and all resistance has ended. In the north, the struggle goes on. There's a lot of bitterness about Britain and its feeble assistance. This is probably the first really major defeat the Allies have suffered and their own press is anything but kind. Things are coming to a head in the Mediterranean instead, they say, and there are fears that Italy will finally remember the 'Rome–Berlin Axis' (of which we heard nothing for the duration of the Finnish war) and join the war on the German side. The Balkans is one of the flashpoints now, a volcano that could erupt at any time.

10 MAY

No, there was no eruption in the Balkans this time, it was all smoke and mirrors. As dawn was breaking this 10 May, German troops moved into Holland, Belgium and Luxembourg 'on the broadest of fronts'.

And the battle that ensues will, according to Hitler's order of the day, decide 'the fate of the German people for the next thousand years'. Of course it's not only the German people's fate that's at stake, but possibly all humanity's. Now the war has *really* started. Germany's justification is the standard one: prevention of an imminent Allied attack. As usual, they say they have documents that provide 'evidence' of such an invasion. What's more, the Germans maintain that Belgium and Holland have not been strictly neutral and intended to allow the deployment of Allied troops on their territory. Bombardments and battles have started with a vengeance. Belgium is reckoned to have better prospects of defending itself than Holland, because it's better fortified. Holland's been partially laid under water. King Leopold has put himself at the head of the Belgian army.

Princess Juliana is expecting her third child. It certainly isn't much fun being a royal mother in times like these. Or a mother of any description.

Last night the British prime minister, Chamberlain, resigned. Churchill took his place.

In the whole of northern Europe Sweden is now the only nation that is neither currently at war, nor has been. But it could be our turn next. Germany is like some malevolent monster that emerges from its cave at regular intervals to pounce on a fresh victim. There *has to* be something wrong with a people that finds itself pitted against the rest of humanity every 20 years or so.

WHIT MONDAY

Ah, so now it's blackout time for all of Sweden. The order has come through right in the middle of the Whit weekend. The south and west of Sweden have already had it for quite a while but from last night the whole country is to be blacked out 'until further notice'. There's also news about the rationing of toilet soap, household cleaning soap, washing powder and margarine. From 26 May, margarine is not to be sold for personal consumption at all.

So far we have rationing of coffee, tea, sugar and margarine, but I expect that's only the start. The current coffee, tea and sugar rations are sufficient for my household, at least.

What a Whit Sunday we had yesterday! Filthy weather, cold – Sture on duty with the army from 6 in the morning to 5 in the afternoon. Karin's come out in strange pustules, presumably triggered by some kind of bacterial infection, so I want to keep her at home. Lars went on a bike ride to Uppsala with Göran and Segerfelt.

15 MAY

Holland surrendered yesterday. Queen Wilhelmina and the government are in London. The children of the Belgian royal family must be there as well.

Belgium is still holding out. Major engagements on the old First World War battlefields. It says in the evening papers that the Maginot Line has been breached somewhere. Whether it's true or not, they've every reason to feel jittery in Paris and London. And the rest of us, for that matter. The German army is proceeding with terrible efficiency. For the first time in the history of the world, parachute troops have been deployed to real effect.

18 MAY

Brussels is under German occupation. The Germans also claim to have broken through a wide stretch of the Maginot Line and to be within 100km of Paris. One dreads opening the newspaper each day.

This morning the new motor vehicle restrictions come into force. Almost all private cars will have to be off the road.

Today was Karin's sixth birthday. Today the Germans reached the English Channel. And today summer arrived, wonderful and painfully lovely to take in, with all one's senses. It really *smelt* like summer today, the air full of scents and the pale green of the leaves on the trees looking fabulous.

For the first time in Karin's life, her father wasn't at home for her birthday. All leave was cancelled from Saturday evening, though Sture got special dispensation to stay at home until Sunday afternoon, when he went off into the spring rain. He hasn't spent a night at home since, and will be sleeping in a tent for the next fortnight. That's to say, the rest of his company will; being Sture, he's arranged to have a roof over his head.

All leave has been cancelled nationwide, and the reason is said to be that the Germans have demanded to be allowed to march through Sweden and the German navy has steamed up through the straits of Øresund. All military personnel the police found on the streets or at places of entertainment on Saturday evening were sent directly to their camps.

God grant that the world will look different by Karin's next birthday! She got a jug with matching glasses for fruit squash, a rain cape and underwear for her doll Margareta, a little doll sitting on a chair, a birthday cake, money from Granny and Grandad [Astrid Lindgren's parents] and from Grandmother [her mother-in-law], a little doll with a pram from Anders, a silver spoon and some chocolate from Matte and Elsa-Lena, sweets from Pelle Dieden and Linnéa. So she was very happy. Anders, Matte and their mothers came round.

In the evening I was out at Anne-Marie and Stellan's at Stora Essingen. We went for a walk round the island in the light of the full moon with the scent of lime blossom and budding bird cherry in our nostrils. Lovely, lovely! But the Germans are advancing by forced march; nothing can stop them.

25 MAY

Our blackout was lifted yesterday, for the time being. In Britain they've more or less imposed a dictatorship. The British are finally starting to realize it's a matter of life and death.

28 MAY

King Leopold surrendered today and 'the Belgian army has ceased to exist'. Reynaud, addressing the French people on the radio, was openly critical of the fact that he took the step alone, without consulting his allies. But I don't suppose he had any choice.

5 JUNE

In Germany, flags will be flown for eight days and bells rung for three in celebration of the battle for Flanders. The battle is 'a bigger Waterloo, a bigger Sedan, a bigger Tannenberg than German history has ever seen'. And this morning they are launching a new offensive. Churchill made a speech in the House of Commons, admitting that the Allies had suffered huge losses of equipment. But at least most of the British Expeditionary Force managed to get back across the Channel in one piece. In the nick of time.

Dunkirk has fallen and the last Allied soldier has left the bloodiest battlefield in world history to an occupying enemy. And the battle for Flanders can go down in history as the largest and possibly most remarkable of human conflicts.

10 JUNE

Today brought two pieces of news: Norway has laid down its weapons and Italy has declared war on France and England. The whole world is ablaze! America's threatened to come into the war if Italy intervenes – so we'll have to wait and see.

14 JUNE

SWASTIKA FLIES ON EIFFEL TOWER said the billboards this evening. The Germans have reached Paris. Deserted streets and shuttered windows met them there. It must be very hard to be Parisian. In Berlin they're ringing bells and waving flags like mad.

16 JUNE

Verdun has fallen. The French army is evidently in total disarray. It's rumoured there's to be a separate peace. Hitler was interviewed by an American journalist and expressed himself very soberly about his war aims.

In the newspaper today there was a short item about Princess Juliana, who gave birth prematurely after escaping to London, and the baby boy later died. A son at last – how terrible that it had to be in circumstances like these. An ironic twist of fate.

18 JUNE

Pauvre France! The French army surrendered yesterday. The whole Maginot Line is surrounded, Paris has fallen into German hands and the enemy has forced its way into about half the country. 'France will accept no ignominious peace,' the papers are saying today, but, but, but! Hitler and Mussolini are meeting today: two hearty lads who can surely cook up a peace to outdo Versailles several times over. It says in *Aftonbladet* that they're thinking of dividing France down the middle, not for ever of course, but for now and for the foreseeable future the country is to be occupied by German and Italian troops. Trust Mussolini to turn up like a vulture to share the spoils. 'Just let me give him a piece of my mind,' as Ingrid from Brofall's maid put it. Poor France! Britain will carry on the fight. 'Carry on' is hardly the right phrase; 'begin' would be more like it, because up to now the British have had an extraordinary knack for avoiding combat. 'The British will fight to the last Frenchman' as usual. But just now it must feel pretty scary to be marooned on that island, waiting for the next lightning attack from Hitler. Because now it'll presumably be Britain's turn.

The worst thing is, soon we won't even be able to wish for a German defeat any more, because the Russians are on the move again. In the last few days they've occupied Lithuania, Latvia and Estonia, on sundry pretexts. And a weakened Germany can only mean one thing for us Nordic nations – that we'll be overrun with Russians. And I think I'd rather say 'Heil Hitler' for the rest of my life than have that happen. I can't think of anything more appalling. I met a Finnish woman out at Elsa Gullander's on Sunday and she told us some dreadful things about the Finnish war and the way the Russians treat their prisoners. Her own brother, just released from captivity, had been beaten until his ears, nose and mouth bled. Another prisoner was shut up in a small room with a 100-watt bulb until he went blind. She seemed absolutely reliable, so it must be true. The most terrible thing of all was when the Russians drove Polish women and children ahead of them towards the Finns. Some of the Finns couldn't bear to shoot them, so they surrendered voluntarily – and now they face court martial in Finland. So do those who couldn't withstand being tortured in the Russian jails and revealed what they knew about the Finnish armed forces. But when red-hot splints are being forced under your nails (which she swore was true), it can't be at all easy to stand firm. The Russians were said to have crucified three Finnish ladies' defence volunteers. She'd heard this but couldn't guarantee it really happened. It was true, however, that the Russians abducted 10 junior volunteers (Finnish girls aged 8–12). Nothing more's been heard of them.

No, o Lord, keep the Russians away from here.

Tomorrow I'm taking the children to Vimmerby. All the schoolchildren have been issued with so-called evacuation tickets, which have cost the state 8 million. But the evacuation train departs at 5 in the morning, so we're travelling on a family ticket at 8 o'clock instead.

21 JUNE

At 15.30 today, Hitler received the French delegation in the railway carriage at the forest of Compiègne where the Armistice was signed in November 1918. We don't yet know the terms of the truce.

In approximately two hours' time – at 1.35 in the early morning of 25 June 1940 – hostilities between Germany and France will cease, and between Italy and France. Italy and France signed the piece of paper confirming their agreement at about 7 this evening in a villa outside Rome, and then Ciano informed Hitler. Six hours later, the ceasefire will come into force and the war in the West will be over. The terms still haven't been made public but it's expected that they will be – in all three countries simultaneously – within 48 hours. In Germany there'll be flags waving and bells clanging for ages, as usual. In France, 25 June will be a national day of mourning.

And what's to come now? *Los gegen England* [Let England have it!] – that's probably going to be the next instalment. In Britain, they're evacuating the children – some of them all the way to Australia, Canada and New Zealand.

Gunnar came home from Finland this evening. A lot of people there expect the Russians will soon be back – and now Finland probably won't be able to defend itself. Then we'll very likely find the Germans wading in to 'protect' us. Will the day really come when the Nordic countries are no longer free? Norway and Denmark have already lost their freedom, of course.

Maybe there are lots of soldiers dying on the western front right now – two hours before the ceasefire. Human stupidity is simply colossal.

The Soviet Union has delivered an ultimatum to Romania, which runs out at midnight tonight. Romania is to give up Bessarabia and two districts in northern Bucovina and allow the use of Constanza [Constanța] and other Black Sea ports as Russian naval bases. Romania has submitted to its demands.

There's an awful lot going on! On Wednesday, British naval forces attacked *French* marine units in the French naval port of Oran in Algeria. The British wanted to stop the French fleet falling into German hands and issued an ultimatum to the French commanders to surrender their ships. In some cases they did this good-naturedly but the commander in Oran refused and there was a violent sea battle. According to Churchill, 'the loss of human life among the French and at the port must have been great'.

Today, as a result of what happened, *diplomatic relations between France and Great Britain have been severed.*

It takes very little to break friendly treaties these days. And once again, Hitler has got what he wants – splits among the Allies.

21 JULY

In a long speech to the German parliament on Friday, Hitler issued a peace ultimatum. He won't get any official response from Britain. The fighting will go on. And in its atrocity it will exceed anything the world has seen before. Germany is better prepared for action than ever and Britain, too, claims to be ready to mobilize on a grand scale. Roosevelt also gave a speech (before Hitler's) encouraging the British to hold out in this battle over 'the continuance of civilization as we know it versus the ultimate destruction of all that we have held dear'.

Today, three free countries ceased to exist – Estonia, Latvia and Lithuania! They were declared independent on 18 November 1918 – 22 years of building up their nations, now declared dead by the Soviet

Union, which has incorporated them as republics. One is simply incapable of feeling sorry any more – but it certainly is a tragedy.

In spite of everything, Finland does at least still have its freedom, for now. Perhaps their struggle was not in vain. The Olympic Games were supposed to start in Helsinki yesterday, had the world been the home of reason and not a madhouse. Instead they are now holding national championships at Helsinki Stadium to honour the memory of fallen Finnish sportsmen.

Lars and I got back from our cycling trip yesterday. We had a wonderful ride through Roslagen and stayed over at Norra Latin's summer hostel on Björkö [island]. We saw so many lovely sights: the roadsides edged with the yellow of lady's bedstraw, the open horizon across the sea at Simpnäs, the full moon over the water and the hostel roof. And the sun blazed down – intense and relentless. We've had no rain in this fateful summer of 1940, everything's looking so parched and burnt and the crops are pretty much failing. That dreadful winter seemed to me to be God's punishment on the human race – is it the same with this drought?

The lord of the world – the wild beast of the Book of Revelations – once an unknown little German artisan, the rehabilitator of his people and (as I and many others see it) annihilator, agent of cultural decline – what is his end to be? Will we at some point have reason to say: *Sic transit gloria mundi*?

I SEPTEMBER

Today it's been a year since the beginning of war. We're starting to get used to it. At least those of us who live in a place where it isn't exactly raining bombs all the time.

A year! Has so much ever happened in a single year before? I haven't written any entries in this war history of mine for a long time now, because nothing particularly sensational has happened recently. Things were so tense between Japan and Britain for a while that we expected war would be declared any time, but the threat seems to have passed for now. Things haven't been going smoothly between Romania and Hungary either, or between Romania and Bulgaria. Romania's had to give up various bits, I think. But the Axis Powers run their affairs the way they want. Greece and Italy have been at each other's throats as well.

The huge German attack on Britain that Hitler announced in his speech in July hasn't exactly turned out as intended. The skies over England are teeming with planes that are dropping bombs as fast as they can, to be sure, but the British are giving more or less as good as they get, and there's been no sign of any invasion of England. At first the Germans were attacking both day and night, but now it's only at night; they dare not risk too many casualties. In both Berlin and London, people are spending hours in shelters overnight. Hamburg is said to have been comprehensively bombed by the British; I doubt there's very much of the port left.

How the food situation is in Britain I don't know, but in Germany they say it's very, very bad. The shortage of fats is hitting particularly hard. I heard of some Germans who were over here and were invited to a smörgåsbord. All they ate was bread and butter, and when their host asked them why they weren't eating anything else they replied that if we in Sweden had experienced what they had, we'd be overjoyed by a meal of bread and butter. I know that in Norway they're getting very scant fare, too. Norwegian feeling towards Sweden is currently hostile, reportedly as hostile as in 1905. This is because we're letting German troop trains pass through – it's an open secret. We're doing that – presumably because we have to – and we've also engaged in some horse-trading with Germany over coal. I expect the Norwegians are also angry because their interned countrymen have allegedly been badly treated.

Finland is in a pretty precarious situation in its foreign policy. Finland's been obliged to let Russian troop trains through to Hangö [Hanko]. And Tanner has left the government, not of his own free will but on the orders of Moscow. So Finland's right of determination has now been considerably curtailed.

In our own little land we aren't that badly affected by all this, in spite of everything. But prices just keep rising. Our coffee ration has to last us six weeks now, rather than five. Last spring I said that if the war wasn't over by the autumn, we just wouldn't be able to bear it any longer. And yet we are! After an unspeakably rainy August – as ridiculously wet as it was dry before that (because there's no moderation in anything this year) – we returned to town last Saturday, and I've rarely been so glad to get back to our place. Despite everything, one still takes an interest in making one's home look nice. It's really smart in the children's room. Karin's got a new chest of drawers and Lars has a reading lamp above the sofa, which is where he sleeps now, while Karin has inherited his splendid bed with the canopy curtains. Pelle Dieden came round, passing on her cold to the kids and grieving for Emil.

A year has gone by! Will we have peace by next 1 September? Adolf claims the war will be over before the end of the month – as the farmer said when the doctor told him the old woman wouldn't last the month: 'It'll be interesting to see how that goes.'

To finish with, a story that tickled me:

A Swede boasts to a Dane about our Swedish neutrality-guarding forces, how reliable and smart, etc. they are, and when he's gone on like that for a while, the Dane says coolly and calmly: 'You should see our Germans.'

11 SEPTEMBER

The punch-up continues. It's total aerial war between Britain and Germany. On 7 September, the Germans launched a terrible mass bombardment of London and since then they've been coming back night after night, dropping bombs on the capital by the ton. There are huge fires burning, which help the Germans find their way. But the British are doing their best to answer them in kind, and tonight they bombed Berlin, setting a lot of buildings on fire including the Reichstag and the academy of art. We don't hear as much about the damage in Germany, but we can be sure the British are far from inactive. The fact is that the populations of both London and Berlin have to spend most of the night in shelters. Ugh! Not an evening passes without me lying in bed and thanking my Heavenly Father that in this country we can still sleep undisturbed. But it's hard thinking about all those who can't.

Oh yes, and King Carol of Romania has abdicated in favour of his son Michael. Madame Lupescu has gone with him into exile and Princess Helena, or the 'queen mother' to use her new title, has returned to Bucharest. It must be exciting to be royal these days.

And we've been issued with ration cards for bread.

21 SEPTEMBER

The air war continues and is horrendous! Ten thousand civilians killed by air bombardments in London alone, Churchill said in a speech the other day. And the Germans have promised even more destructive methods. They expect the war to end by this autumn and Ribbentrop has just been in Rome. The partition of Africa was apparently under discussion. Under the 'new order', only Germany, Italy and Spain will have any say in that area. The expectation is, incidentally, that Spain will enter the war on the side of the Axis Powers any day now. Although one would think that poor country had already had enough after its civil war in 1936–37.

In Norway, the Germans are rebuilding the roads for all they are worth and concentrating their troops up in the north as a salutary memento mori to the Russians.

On the 15th of the month I started my secret 'defence work', which is so secret that I daren't even write about it here. I've been in the job for a week. And it's become completely clear to me that, as things stand, there's no country in Europe left so untouched by the impact of the war as here, in spite of a considerable rise in prices, rationing and increased unemployment. We live sumptuously here, as foreigners see it. To my mind, our rations are so generous that anyone who bought all that we are entitled to would end up in dire financial straits.

And yesterday we had hot water – and will be getting it two days a week. Kar de Mumma's column in *Svenska Dagbladet* today gave us his picture of events:

[Swedish press cutting pasted here: extract from a comic column.]

From Monday, bread will be rationed too, so now we'll have to take our coupons with us to the restaurant, as well. Things could turn out like in this Danish cartoon.

[Cutting from Dagens Nyheter, *1940: the Danish
Post Office is to administer bread coupons, giving
customers their change in small-denomination stamps.
A Danish cartoonist imagines the scene.]*

It's extraordinary, the way one can grow accustomed to simply anything! I was wondering the other day whether a time will ever come when it strikes us as unnatural to see a 'Shelter' sign down in our peaceful entrance halls. At the moment it actually feels perfectly in order that there are rooms everywhere whose sole function is to protect human beings if other human beings happen to start chucking bombs at them. So when I see the sign in the hall with its blue letters saying 'Shelter' every time I go out, or see the notice in the lift that it is not to be used during an air-raid alert, I don't react in the slightest. If only we could hope to hear our grandchildren ask one day: 'Shelter – what does that mean?'

26 SEPTEMBER

Yesterday Terboven, the German War Commissioner for Norway, addressed the Norwegian people on the radio, and anybody still holding out hope that Norway would be able to control its own affairs was soon disappointed. The royal family have been deposed and are not allowed to return to Norway, nor is the Nygaardsvold government. All political parties are forbidden in Norway except for National Unity, i.e. Quisling's party. So the traitor Quisling has won, and is shortly expected to take his place in the new Council of State, where the other appointments that have been announced are all fellows of the same stamp as Quisling. Poor King Haakon and Olav and Märtha! Märtha and her three children went over to America a while back, at the invitation of President Roosevelt; Haakon and Olav must be in England. And today in Denmark there was a huge turnout to celebrate King Christian's 70th birthday. Denmark seems to have got off more lightly after its invasion than Norway, though they both have equally restricted rights of self-determination.

Other news is that the Japanese have marched into Indochina and the French have apparently bombarded Gibraltar – this misery is extending everywhere. We'll have to see whether, once the presidential election is over, America joins in the game as well.

29 SEPTEMBER

Now Japan's made a pact with Italy and Germany which amounts to Japan joining the Axis Powers if any other major power (i.e. America) sides with Britain.

Sture just said he thinks the war will be over by Christmas. *He who lives will see* [in English].

[*Cutting from* Dagens Nyheter *on 4 October with picture of the Norwegian flag and news that it, and the parliament, are to be abolished.*]

13 OCTOBER

No, it was a lie! The intention is clearly for the Norwegians to keep their flag.

Last Saturday they introduced coupons for bacon and ham, and then (yesterday) we were all braced for butter coupons, so I – for the children's sake – stocked up on 3 or 4 kg. But there was no word of butter coupons. So I'm left with a refrigerator full of the stuff.

In occupied France they get *200 grams of butter* a month, according to information in our letters. The letters also refer to starvation in Belgium. Everything, clothes and food, gets sent to Germany, if the letter-writers are to be believed. It makes one feel quite hopeless, sitting at work and reading them. All these occupied countries, whether it's the Baltic states under Russia or the countries Germany has suppressed, are suffering badly under the foreign yoke. In Estonia (and presumably Latvia, Lithuania and Poland, too; though I haven't read any letters from there) nobody is allowed to own more than 30 hectares of ground. If you have even half a hectare more, it has to be nationalized. On 1 October, all goods went up by 40–50%; the previous day there was complete panic in the shops, according to the letter-writers. People aren't allowed to have big apartments any more; each individual is only allocated a certain amount of space; the rest is occupied by 'guests', as they're called, who pay no rent. People daren't write too much in their letters, but promise 'I'll tell you all about it when I see you.' Russian has replaced English in schools; the kids are expected to learn 1,000 Russian words in a year. The last confirmations have taken place – and one girl was worried that they wouldn't be allowed to celebrate Christmas this year.

In the Dutch letters I read about the blackout. Under the new regulations, no one's allowed out after 9 (or perhaps it was 10?), or before 4 in the morning. If you have guests, they either have to clear off home early or bring a blanket and bed down in a corner. Cue much flirting and laughter (according to my Dutch informant) when the guests have to find a berth until 4 o'clock comes round. Ah well, even this year of grace 1940 has its compensations!

I still think the Norwegians deserve our pity most. There's been a clothes collection for Norway and I scraped together a few things, among them my old ski boots which I bought on that memorable cross-country hike, God knows how many years ago; it must have been 1924.

In Finland things are superficially calm, I suppose, but there's no real sense of security. Finland, like Sweden, now admits to allowing the transit of German soldiers going on leave but there's a rumour going round that the Germans are staying in the country. According to one report, which naturally can't be true, there are currently 100,000 Germans in Finland. Be that as it may, Finland is investing all its hopes in Germany now, for protection against Russia; how justified they are in this remains to be seen. Anyway, the Russian peril is a constant, menacing threat for both Finland and Sweden – and right now we are concentrating our defence forces up on the Finnish border.

There's trouble brewing in the Balkans. Romania and Hungary can't agree. Germany has stationed a lot of troops in Romania, apparently hoping to inject a bit of life into the Romanian army, which is rotten to the core. This has led Britain to threaten to break off diplomatic relations with Romania. Little Greece is quaking in its boots. Britain will soon be opening the 'Burma Road'. I haven't a clue what that means, but it sounds ominous.

Sweden is still at peace. Almost every letter includes a sigh of gratitude for this miracle. Because it really is a miracle. And Sweden is the Shangri-La where you can still get food, cakes and chocolate. On all their postcards to Finland, Finns who are over here on visits are in raptures over the chocolate, fruit and cakes. The fruit trees froze last winter in Finland, and Estonia too, so there's been hardly any fruit this year.

Words can't express how pitiful it is to read letters every day containing desperate pleas from the poor Jews for visas and entry permits to one country or another. They roam the globe, forever rootless and homeless, from what I can understand. So many are writing just at the moment with New Year wishes, enquiring after relations who have settled in Buenos Aires or died when a bomb hit Tel Aviv.

And it feels strange to read letters from people who are writing about women and children they know *personally* who have been killed in bombing raids. As long as you're only reading about it in the paper you can sort of avoid believing it, but when you read in a letter that 'both Jacques's children were killed in the occupation of Luxembourg' or something like that, it suddenly brings it home, quite terrifyingly. Poor human race: when I read their letters I'm staggered by the amount of sickness and distress, grief, unemployment, poverty and despair that can be fitted into this wretched earth.

But the Lindgren family is all right! Today I took my well-nourished children to the cinema to see *Young Tom Edison*. We live in our nice, cosy home; yesterday we had lobster and liver pâté for dinner, today ox tongue and red cabbage; hard-boiled eggs and goose liver on our smörgåsbord (we've Sture to thank for that extravagance). But of course it's only on Saturdays and Sundays that such gluttony's allowed, and even then it makes me feel guilty, thinking about the French and their 200g of butter a month.

I'm earning 385 kronor a month, thanks to the war. Sture (thanks to the war) is virtually a director at M. [Motormännens Riksförbund, the Swedish motorists' association] and it's probably only a matter of time before he's officially appointed. At the board meeting on the 27th they're discussing whether to give him a pay rise. We're far too fortunate. And I'm so grateful; naturally I try to impress my gratitude on God, so He will continue His kindness in the future and hold His hand over me and mine.

29 OCTOBER

Yesterday morning, Italy went to war with Greece. Or, as one might expect, 'Greece bears total responsibility for the commencement of hostilities' – of course. Italy had merely issued a request to be allowed to use some strategic points on Greek territory to pep up its stagnating offensive in the eastern Mediterranean. But lo and behold, Greece wouldn't agree to that, making the Italian newspapers declare it 'the last straw'. The question now is whether Britain can do anything to save Greece. The Mediterranean fleet is certainly strong, but in the air Britain already has enough to do, defending its empire in North Africa. Now the battle for the Mediterranean will get going in earnest, I daresay. Poor Greece! Yugoslavia can't do a thing, because if it does, it will immediately be attacked by Italy and Germany. Romania obviously can't do anything, Bulgaria doesn't *want* to. That leaves Turkey, which definitely has reason to intervene, but the geography isn't on their side.

Dear little Hitler has been zooming about from one country to another for a while now. First he was in France, meeting old Pétain to lay down the broad outlines of a separate peace with France, then he went to meet Franco to persuade him to drag Spain into the war on the Axis Powers' side (I don't think he succeeded though; Spain can scarcely endure a British blockade), then he was off to Florence to see Mussolini and cook up this Greek business, i.e. it was all planned well in advance.

Here in Sweden last week, on 24 October, we suffered the worst accident that has ever befallen us, I think, in terms of human lives lost. At Armasjärvi up by the Finnish border, 46 young servicemen died when a ferry carrying 102 sank in the bad storm.

6 NOVEMBER

Franklin Roosevelt has been re-elected president of the USA for the third time, which is unprecedented in American history. They thought Willkie had a good chance but when it came to the crunch, Roosevelt won a resounding victory. Rejoicing in Britain, as this means better prospects of America joining the war.

This is what the first ration cards in this war looked like. Coupon A8, crossed through, went on margarine, I seem to remember.

*[An undated and unidentified newspaper article plus four
little coupons with the names of the four family members.]*

Other than that I'm sure it was sugar and coffee we used these first
emergency cards for, and soap and washing powder. To date we still
have cards for sugar, coffee, tea, cocoa, flour and bread, washing powder,
bacon and ham, I'm pretty sure that's it. We're quite short of coffee
now, since the rationing period was increased to seven weeks from
the original four. Other rations seem fairly generous to me, though I
recently read a letter from a woman who was complaining that 'there's
not much sugar and very little flour, and hardly any bacon at all'.
However, people have been stockpiling butter, and today there's not a
knob of butter to be had in the whole town. It would be better if they
brought in coupons for butter, too. There are whispers that there's only
one theory which can explain the shortages of one thing and another,
and it's that the Germans are commandeering provisions from us – and
I think it must be true, despite all the government's emphatic denials.

At work today we heard some alarming news via a letter from that
little Baby Jesus, Sven Stolpe, to a woman in Finland. He said that the
Germans are censoring post from Finland; letters that he had received
were clearly stamped with *'Deutsches Wehrkommando, Rovaniemi'*
[German Armed Forces Command, Rovaniemi]. If this is true – and
there have been indications before – then Germany is plainly leading all
the Nordic countries by the nose, whether we will or no. And of course
it's happening. You can tell from so many of the letters that pretty much
the entire Swedish nation is aware of the fact. What strange political
constellations can come about! The Nordic nations are democratic with
heart and soul and can't possibly reconcile themselves to dictatorship
on the German model. Germany and Russia were originally mortal
enemies, or at any rate, their respective ideologies were absolutely alien

to each other. But they're allies now, all the same. It seems to me our whole country is overwhelmingly pro-British – but we're nonetheless obliged to throw in our lot with the Germans. Germany's presence in Finland is viewed by the Finns as protection against the Russians, but if one takes that to its logical conclusion it would mean Russia and Germany falling out and Finland and Germany, in all likelihood with Sweden's help, waging war on Russia together – and by going to war on Germany's side, making an enemy of Britain. Dear oh dear, what a muddle!

Little Greece is fighting pluckily and seems to be making some gains, perhaps largely because the Italians are even worse soldiers than the Greeks.

And now the first snow has arrived and the second winter of the war is upon us – with its attendant tears, privations, wants, misery and anxieties for all the people of Europe.

IO NOVEMBER

The nice old gentleman with the umbrella who was always running late, our 1938 dove of peace, hugely admired by us all because he really did seem to have found a way of avoiding war – that is, Neville Chamberlain – passed away last night. So he didn't live to see how this spectacle would end, which is probably just as well. I shall never forget those alarming days of September 1938, when the clouds of war were massing more threateningly than ever, and how wonderful we thought it was when Chamberlain resolutely stuck his umbrella under his arm and flew off to Munich. Things calmed down, we thought the millennium was at hand and Chamberlain had the esteem of a whole world – apart possibly from the Czechoslovaks. But within the year, Herr Hitler was poised again – and this time even Chamberlain could see that being nice wasn't enough. But it was rather late in the day by then. He has had to suffer an immense amount of blame ever since and has come to be seen as the personification of democracy's incompetence. Germany's secret weapon – that's Chamberlain, as some wag put it. And after the Munich assassination attempt and the German accusations that the British were behind it, people said it was obvious Chamberlain had set it up – because it happened ten minutes late. Be that as it may, he was a fine old man and I'm glad he has escaped from this troublesome planet of ours. Perhaps God will give him a nice little place in Heaven – 'blessed are the meek' – where he can sit under his umbrella undisturbed.

15 NOVEMBER

Yesterday I turned 33. Children and husband ceremonially presented me with a bag and a sewing box in the morning. Karin attired in her pale-blue dance tunic. We had duck and red cabbage and a cake for dinner; there wasn't the slightest trace of belt-tightening. From home they sent me a splendid box of assorted foodstuffs including 2kg of butter. That's the best birthday present anyone could wish to receive just now. It's literally impossible to buy butter in Stockholm at present because so many people are hoarding it. We're only allowed to buy small pats each time. But there's plenty of butter in the rest of the country, I think.*

Since I last wrote, two things have happened: a dreadful earthquake in Romania left tens of thousands dead, and Molotov went to see Hitler. The Swedish people and presumably other peoples, too, are racking their brains about possible results of the visit. We're pretty convinced the Germans are capable of the most nefarious horse-trading if need be, but we *assume* it's about the Balkans, while presumably the Balkans hope and believe it's about us.

* No, we sent loads to Finland, presumably for the German troops' use.

17 NOVEMBER

Albert Engström died last night. The third of our greats, first Selma Lagerlöf, then Heidenstam and now Albert, all in one year. He was the son of Grandmother's cousin, 'if that's anything to boast about,' as Mrs V. [presumably Alice Viridén] said.

23 NOVEMBER

The Greeks have actually driven all the Italians out of their country; battles are raging in Albania. I expect Germany will soon have to intervene and help its distressed Axis partner, which has never been able to get through a war unaided. In Britain they say: 'Fair's fair. In the last world war, *we* had Italy as an ally, so now it's Germany's turn.' King Boris of Bulgaria went to see Hitler, Hungary has made a pact with the Axis Powers. Turkey's preparing for war.

Finland seems very jumpy. We've seen reports in the letters that some places in the Hangö [Hanko] area have been evacuated, including Ekenäs. (Lies!) Some letters even said the Germans had pulled out of Finland again, which really worried us. But Brita Wrede said yesterday that her brother-in-law from Finland said the Russians were also withdrawing from Hangö [Hanko]. Dare we interpret this as an indication that Hitler and Molotov have made some kind of – dare we call it 'gentleman's agreement', to remove troops from Finland because they are more urgently needed elsewhere? We'll have to see. The other day I had a letter from a German major-general staying at the Grand Hotel, Stockholm, to an Oberleutnant at a hotel in Vasa [Vaasa], containing among other things a photo of the sender with the words [in German] 'In grateful memory of past work in Lapland autumn 1940' written on it. He also writes that Mannerheim awarded him 'Commander of the White Rose of Finland'– I'd like to know what for. He goes on to hope that the war will bring him back together with the addressee in some other place – 'that would be very nice'. I think it would be 'very nice' if the war ended, instead.

Last night I read *Tyskt väsen och svensk lösen* [*German Nature and Swedish Watchword*], Fredrik Böök's pamphlet, which has caused a lot of controversy. As Eyvind Johnson put it in a letter to Diktonius, Böök is such a fair-weather friend. I reckon he turns whichever way the wind is blowing, and just now there are terrible gales blowing across the northern countries. I think Böök is pretty much right in what he says about the psychological roots of Nazism, but as for his blind, naive faith (assuming it's genuine) in the advantages for us of becoming part of a new order after these truths of the last days, I can't share that. I could never put my faith in a regime which created the concentration camps in Oranienburg and Buchenwald, which permitted, and backed, the pogroms in the autumn of 1938 and which sentences a Norwegian girl to a year in prison for tearing up a photograph of the Führer.

30 NOVEMBER

One whole year ago, a year to the day, the Finnish war started, and what a day!! It was the start of a long succession of them, filled with agony and despair, probably culminating in that hard day of peace when I expect all of us here in Sweden were painfully aware of how bitter they must feel towards us in Finland – in spite of all we'd done to help them. But as for the most crucial and important thing – active intervention – we didn't do that, even though almost all of us, when feelings were running at their highest, took an extremely activist stance. But our wise government, which at the time we all scorned and loathed, held us back – and subsequent world events have proved them right, of course. But we didn't know it last winter, and we felt awful, knowing that the Finnish soldiers were fighting alone, stretched way beyond human capacity. I wonder whether any people has ever felt so deeply for another as we did then; we were in the grip of an unrequited love for Finland and in our love and desperation we gave Finland everything we could possibly think of – money, hundreds of millions of kronor, if you add it all up, arms, ammunition, clothes, food, bottled blood, skis, horse blankets, ambulances, medical aid, woollens that we knitted like mad, wedding rings and goodness knows what besides. Here in Sweden we took in thousands upon thousands of children and the factories worked weekends for Finland, with people donating a day's wages a month, and so on ad infinitum. Yet even so we constantly had a dreadful sense of not doing enough. But the bitterness the Finns most certainly felt towards us when peace was made has definitely faded now and on the whole I think the Finns are actually grateful to Sweden, because when all is said and done, without Sweden the outcome of the war would probably have been even worse. I believe that for as long as I live I shall remember Finland's war of 1939–40, its 'Winter of Honour', when a whole people struggled for its freedom beyond the limit of its abilities. Finland's war, Finland's soldiers fighting in their white camouflage suits, the unbelievable cold, the unbelievable battle on the Karelian Isthmus, at Suomussalmi, at Petsamo it's all still so vivid in our minds that there's no comparing it to anything else, and the emotions we felt that winter are beyond all comparison, too.

Things are difficult between Sweden and Norway. That is, our feelings for the Norwegians haven't changed, but there are recurring indications that they feel a lot of rancour towards us. They think we let Germans come through here during their war against Norway. And 34 railway carriages are certainly said to have passed through Sweden carrying 'medical orderlies' and food supplies during the war – I don't know if that report is true, but the Norwegians must have some basis for believing what they do. The Germans, of course, are doing their best to stir up the bitterness. We hear awful things from Norway, there really does seem to be a reign of terror there, but the Norwegians refuse to be cowed. Or at any rate, it looks as if the National Unity Party and Quisling won't be able to keep the people in order. Quisling was down in Berlin the other day. God grant that the Germans realize that sort of thing won't work on the Norwegians.

Hitler made another speech today, but he actually sounds a bit weary. And when he says Germany's going to win, militarily and economically, I don't think he sounds very convincing. One of the Swedish journalists invited to Germany recently told Sture that the German people don't believe in victory any more. Time is working in Britain's favour as usual, and seeing as the much-vaunted German invasion hasn't happened, one might almost start to doubt Germany's chances of winning.

Not to mention Italy's! Greece has driven the Italians further and further back into Albania and things are looking dismal for the Italian forces in North Africa, too. Marshal Badoglio, the chief of the general staff, and various other top dogs have left their posts, which is generally a sure sign of weakness. Mussolini's said to be pretty depressed and according to today's *Aftonbladet*, Count Ciano is being blamed for the failure of the Greek venture.

Oh yes, and I forgot to write that Kallio has stood down as president of Finland on the grounds of ill health. That man of honour, he has the deep respect of his people. Ryti is touted as his likeliest successor, but there's talk of Kivimäki and possibly Paasikivi, too. I'm sure it'll be Ryti, though.

21 DECEMBER

The day before yesterday, the 19th, President Kallio 'journeyed to the place from which none return'. Ryti had just been elected and Kallio and his wife were going to their house in Nivala. They were accompanied to the station by the residents of Helsinki, with Mannerheim and Ryti at their head. 'The March of the Björneborg Regiment' was played, the presidential couple's route was lined with flaming brands – then he collapsed, their fine little president, and would have sunk to the ground if Mannerheim had not put out an arm to support him. He was carried into a railway carriage, where he breathed his last. A noble Finnish heart had stopped beating – and his parting from his people could hardly have been more dramatic. He was much loved in Sweden too, we can see that in today's letters.

In the Libyan desert, battles have been raging for some time now between the British and Italians – and the Italians are hard pressed. Plus how can you wage war in a desert, to which every crumb of food, every drop of water and all ammunition has to be transported such vast distances? What's more, according to today's communiqué the British fleet has moved up the Adriatic, putting the Italian troops in Albania in a disastrous position and meaning that a British invasion of Italy is now conceivable, at least. Sture told a funny story about the poor Italians (in the press no jokes about the Italians are permitted until the Italian trade agreement is concluded). In France there are French and Italian troops on either side of the demarcation line. And now, Sture claims, the French have put up big notices: 'Greeks halt! French territory begins here!'

There's been a shocking accident in Bofors [armaments factory], or Björkborn works to be precise. Some TNT caught light and as a result there was a dreadful explosion and a devastating fire. Eight dead. We're not being told the extent of the destruction, the newspapers aren't allowed to give details.

28 DECEMBER

Christmas has come and gone, our second wartime Christmas! And there *was* no bombing on Christmas night after all! No air-raid sirens in either Berlin or London.

Here in Sweden, Christmas was celebrated just as usual, as far as I can gather. We stuffed ourselves, just as usual. We must be the only nation in Europe able to do that, at least to that degree.

We, the Lindgrens, spent Christmas in Näs as usual. Sture, newly appointed director at M., insisted we travel second class, so the journey was no trouble at all. On the 26th Sture and I came back (I have a job to go to as well, after all) but the children are staying on for now. We saw Inger Ingvarsdotter for the first time. We were all together for dinner on Christmas Eve, Sammel Agust's [Samuel August] and Hanna's children, grandchildren and all the in-laws.

I think almost everyone here in Sweden feels, just I do this Christmas 1940, that it's a pure, undeserved, unparalleled state of grace which allowed us to celebrate Christmas in peace and quiet in our own homes. Many have had to spend Christmas in the camps where they are stationed. But the ladies' defence volunteers went round handing out Christmas presents and I know there's been a festive atmosphere in the camps, too.

Father [Astrid's father-in-law] hasn't had a happy Christmas, though. He's in a lot of pain now and yesterday they took him by boat and ambulance from Furusund to the Bethany Foundation nursing home in Stocksund. He's a mere shadow of his former self and can't have much longer to live. (†30 December 1940.)

As for the war, nothing particularly startling is happening at the moment except that things are rapidly going to pot for the Italians. Churchill made a speech to the Italian people, pointing out that one man, and one man only, has hurled them to their destruction.

A funny story: malicious tongues in Berlin have it that Quisling went to see Hitler and asked him to promise to let Quisling call the book he's writing about his struggle for power 'Mein Kämpflein' ['My Little Struggle'].

'Unhappy things still happen. Even in our time.' [Quotation from Johan Lindström Saxon's ballad about Elvira Madigan]. At the moment, a proportion of the Swedish population is focused on the trial of Olle Möller, who's accused of the kidnap, rape and murder on 1 December of 10-year-old Gerd Johansson.

This evening I finished reading *Henne fick jag aldrig möta* [*The Woman I Never Met*], which Hans has just published.

1941

The Lindgren family at Vulcanusgatan, 1941.

A new year has begun with a new sales tax, butter rationing and some strict austerity measures. We embarked on our austerity last night by having supper with Alli and the Gullanders, some lobster and assorted other treats. And a visit to Karl Gerhard's New Year's revue, with grave words from K.G. at midnight about 'a free Sweden', and everybody joining in the national anthem.

Things don't feel at all the same as they did this time last year, when we were dreading what 1940 might bring. That's to say, there's every reason for dreading the future now, too, but it just doesn't seem the same to us.

In other respects the world looks even sadder than it did last New Year – Norway is an even greater tragedy than Finland was (Ronald Fangen is reported to have been admitted to a mental hospital, broken by ghastly 'cross-examination' resulting from a newspaper article. The Oxford Group has been given an ultimatum to actively align itself with the new regime or face a ban.)

There's less and less food in Europe, and it's the same with fuel.

Roosevelt made a speech the other day that was received with great satisfaction in Britain, silence in Berlin and vocal bitterness in Italy, which declares that it has 'lost patience' with the USA. It'll be amusing to see what they do when they lose it definitively. Word now has it that Italy's motto is: 'We came when we saw who had conquered.'

If only this New Year could bring us peace! God grant that it will.

So that's that!

The British are the masters of North Africa, Bardia fell a few days ago with tremendous losses for the Italians and it's bound to be Tobruk next. The German air force is allegedly going to be deployed, but the British say it's already too late. There's also talk of German passage through Bulgaria down to Greece. As long as that doesn't mean the Russians have agreed to that in return for a free hand in other places.

Nothing in particular's happening in the big war but I'll still write this entry so I can have a little moan about the general discomfort the whole business is spreading over existence. Did there have to be two perishingly cold winters in a row, just because we're short of coke? It's flipping freezing, outdoors and in! There's been a really harsh cold spell all January and I reckon our flat is around 15–16°. And it's going to get worse, our caretaker promised this evening when I grumbled. In the detached houses out in the suburbs it can only be about 10–12°. If only spring would come soon! The whole of Europe is cold and starving. Well, we're not starving. But they say that in Paris it's as bad as during the siege of 1870–71. One potato costs 5 francs. There are crows and hawks for sale in the markets. Here, we're collecting sugar for Norway and Finland, saving it up from our rations. How lucky we are to be in a situation that means we can help. We're also sponsoring children affected by the war in Finland and Norway, paying them 30 kronor a month. Good grief, there are people everywhere in need of help! Our own men on military service, among others.

Roosevelt and the Pope are said to be concocting peace plans, but I don't suppose they'll come to anything.

A virulent strain of influenza is going round Sweden and in places it's almost as bad as the Spanish flu.

The intervals between our coffee rations are to be increased; I expect we'll soon be getting a bare minimum. I saw one newspaper was predicting meat rationing come the summer.

Tobruk fell a few days ago. The bombardments of Britain and Germany are continuing. Hitler and Mussolini had a meeting.

A story:

Hitler was standing in a hall with a good echo, practising his speech.

He yelled: *Wer beherrscht die grosse Welt?*

The echo answered: *Roosevelt.*

Wer macht den Frieden? –

Eden.

Wo soll die grosse Revolution beginnen?

Innen.

Wer ist die grösste Nation?

Zion.

[Who rules the great world?

The echo answered: Roosevelt.

Who makes peace?

Eden.

Where should the grand revolution begin?

Inside.

Which is the greatest nation?

Zion.]

Then Hitler had had enough.

(Apologies for any spelling mistakes in the above.)

Lars and Göran started dancing classes yesterday. There'll always be dancing – regardless of minor world wars.

That reminds me – in Romania these past few days there's been a punch-up that looks pretty much like a civil war. They say that ex-king Carol, who's in Spain, tried to take his own life.

I FEBRUARY

I cut the pictures overleaf out of *Se* magazine, which Sture brought home with him today. I'd almost forgotten the existence of Poland. But when I read about these poor Jews I'm seized by a hatred of the Germans, who think they have the *right* to trample other peoples underfoot.

> [Press cutting from Se, no. 5 1941: 'Jewish cities behind high stone walls'. Photos of: a wall in Lublin; segregated tram carriages for Jews in Kraków; two elderly women wearing armbands with the Star of David; three women selling the yellow armbands.]

> [Next page, captioned by Astrid: 'And from the same issue of Se – Lindgren family news': picture of Sture, newly appointed head of the Swedish motorists' association, and a paragraph about growing membership and the use of wood gas as wartime fuel.]

9 FEBRUARY

I thought this was a good leader so I pasted it in.

> [Press cutting from Dagens Nyheter, 8 February 1941: 'Benghazi'. What is happening in Africa? The concept of Lebensraum.]

We won the military patrol race [at the Nordic World Ski Championships] in Cortina, beating Germany and Italy and Switzerland and Finland. It's splendid being able to show the Germans what sort of soldiers we have in this country.

Things have gone totally to pot for the Italians. God, what soldiers. The British are masters of all Libya and fighting continues in Eritrea and Abyssinia. The 'Lion of Judah', Haile Selassie, is with the British and preparing to resume his throne, and the Abyssinians are making common cause with the British against the Italians.

What will Germany do? The whole world is in suspense, waiting for the invasion attempt on Britain, which everyone thinks *must* come this spring. And when it happens – well, then the fate of the world will be decided in a day, a few hours. And then I'll even bring myself to listen to the news, something I long since gave up doing on a daily basis.

'The Germans are getting less and less snooty in Stockholm,' I read in one of my letters yesterday. And the fact is, I think they've had to tone down their cockiness. And maybe we've grown a bit more confident – thanks to our unprecedented armaments, which are probably nothing compared to the great powers', but which still weigh in our favour. 'Angels and Fritzes are both courting Svea,' another letter said. Yes, well, as long as they leave us in peace – amen!

3 MARCH

Bulgaria has joined the Tripartite Pact and German troops have been sent in.

Today is the first anniversary of the terrible Finno-Russian peace. This time a year ago was agonizing. In recent days I've been reading two books about last year's war, which has already gone down in history. *Ärans vinter* [*Winter of Honour*] by Håkan Mörne and *Tragedy in France* by André Maurois. They're both utterly gripping. Finland's winter war and France's collapse on those warm May and June days of 1940 – we'll remember them both as long as we live. It's horrifying to read how completely unprepared for this war France was, and Britain too – and how well prepared they were in Germany. Maurois writes: 'It was terrible to realize (…) that a mighty civilization saw itself doomed to perish simply because five thousand tanks and ten thousand aeroplanes, which could easily have been built or bought, were not acquired in time.'

The current situation is one of awaiting disaster. In just the last few days submarine attacks have really intensified and Britain has lost a lot of tonnage. But American aid is increasing and today's *Allehanda* says 'it's hard to see how they (the USA) can cite one formal legal provision after another to stop on the brink of war's abyss'.

On Saturday evening, Mother Svea suddenly and strangely called up large numbers of her sons – and now there is all manner of speculation as to why. Things have been calm for so long that we thought all danger was more or less past, but apparently not. It's true that the government communiqué says it's just to test the effectiveness of our defence readiness, but nobody believes that. Rumour has it that

Germany's made the most outrageous demands, including part of our navy, but nobody really knows anything. I simply haven't the energy to be as nervous and worried as last winter and spring. I don't give a damn and am much more concerned about Karin's raised temperature and tuberculin tests.

The call-ups on Saturday are very worrying, actually. They're extremely comprehensive – a partial general mobilization. Jenny Tanner wrote yesterday to her husband, Väinö Tanner, that things are 'as tense as they were last April, with pressure from the same quarter'. But others seem to think the threat is from Russia. And one letter cheerily claimed the Japanese government had issued an ultimatum that the Japanese fleet be allowed through the Göta Canal [in Sweden].

It's miserable for those called up earlier, who were expecting to be relieved but can now see no prospect of release. Mrs Fåhreus's husband came home from Norrland on Saturday and he's got to go straight back on Monday. A whole contingent from [infantry regiment] 15, who had just been demobbed after six months' service and were on the train south, were ordered to get out at a station and go back. Some were in tears. I'm sure there were tears for Ingegerd, too, who was expecting to be taken to her new home in Skövde at Easter. But now he [her husband Ingvar] has been sent off somewhere in his motherland, so I suppose she'll have to stay at home. Meanwhile Inger's growing all the time and Ingvar hardly gets to see her. But people aren't supposed to be happy or content, it seems.

Britain has suffered its most intensive bombing yet, these past few nights, and this is seen as a prelude to the long-anticipated total invasion.

Thousands of fatalities. The Germans say they're going to reduce England to a heap of rubble. 'This little bit of earth, this England!' No, it mustn't happen!

27 MARCH

Yesterday, or it might have been the day before, the Yugoslav government allied itself to the Axis Powers – and today there are big headlines in the evening papers saying that young King Peter has taken power, Prince Paul has fled and the government has been toppled. The Yugoslav people are rejoicing – they don't want to join Germany. We'll have to see what this all amounts to. There'll probably be war between Germany and Yugoslavia. Turkey is still outside – cheering for Greece. It's going to be awfully interesting to follow developments in the Balkans. Romania and Bulgaria are obedient tools of Germany – it really is marvellous that Yugoslavia is digging in its heels.

Here in the Nordic countries things are still critical, I imagine. Per Albin [Hansson] made a reassuring speech on the radio, which seems to have had the opposite effect. Military letters apparently show (I heard today, though I haven't seen confirmation) that an armed German merchant fleet came within the 30-km limit round Gotland and was gently but firmly driven off by the Swedish navy.

A profoundly sad Jewish letter, a document of its time, crossed my desk today. A Jew who had recently arrived here in Sweden sent a fellow Jew in Finland an account of the transporting of Jews from Vienna to Poland. I believe 1,000 Jews a day were forcibly transported to Poland in the most shocking conditions. Some sort of instruction arrives by post and the individual concerned has to leave home, taking very little money and a minimal amount of luggage. Conditions on the days leading up to transportation, during the journey and on arrival in Poland were such that the letter-writer didn't want to describe them. He had a brother among the unfortunates. It is apparently Hitler's intention to make Poland into one big ghetto where the poor Jews are to perish from hunger and squalor. They are not even able to wash, for example. Poor, wretched people! Surely the God of Israel must intervene soon? How *can* Hitler think one can treat one's own fellow human beings like that? Sture met a Norwegian yesterday who was totally convinced that Germany's going to collapse within a couple of months. But I expect that's just wishful thinking.

6 APRIL

This morning, German troops invaded Yugoslavia and Greece! It wasn't unexpected, that's for sure. Ever since King Peter's coup the situation's been growing more and more tense. After all, the Serbs have never given way to coercion. The tension will be almost unbearable as we wait to see whether things will go as rapidly for Germany in the Balkans as they did in Norway, Holland, Belgium and France. And to see how the Italians in Albania will fare with Greece on one side and Yugoslavia on the other. Hitler issued one of his usual bombastic and pathetic orders of the day.

[Press cutting of Hitler's orders of the day to 'Soldiers on the south-eastern front', translated into Swedish. Unidentified newspaper source. Plus two shorter cuttings: Adua in Abyssinia falls to British forces; British admiralty vs. Axis Powers losses in the sea war, in tonnage.]

It *was* rapid! Yugoslavia is no more. 'Croatia' has been declared independent; as for the rest, it's one big mess that I can't work out. The Serbian army's been decimated. In Greece, the Germans reached Salonika several days ago. Any day now the Germans and British will engage in Greece. In Africa, the Germans' arrival has turned to war, to Britain's disadvantage.

CONTINUED ON EASTER DAY

Damn and blast! Just the other day we were so pleased that Yugoslavia was putting up resistance and taking back power from the pro-German government – and now there barely seems to be a country called Yugoslavia. Things move fast in our time. The vultures are now converging from all directions for their share of the spoils – Hungary, which is actively participating in the war, Bulgaria and Romania. As I understand it, Yugoslavia's in a state of total collapse. Greece still seems to be holding out and in the southern part of the country we hope the British are at the ready. But for now the Germans are in another of those periods that make us think they're invincible. But everything will be decided in the Atlantic, so they say. Britain's loss of tonnage is pretty vast. But there's one thing for sure, if this goes on much longer, Europe will starve to death. I reckon that before long, Portugal and Sweden will be the only ones with any food.

Just imagine us still not being at war. How can it be possible? Here, we've seen one country after another dragged into the fire, but Sweden is *still going strong* [in English].

This autumn, after ten years at Vulcanusgatan, we're moving to an expensive and very nice flat in Dalagatan. It feels pretty awful to be embarking on that sort of undertaking at a time when one can't believe the future will ever settle back into the calm normality of before. But we'll only be on the first floor, so perhaps the bombs won't penetrate that far down.

28 APRIL

The Greeks are plainly on their last legs. The king and the government have left Athens, and there've been indications from various quarters these past few days that the Germans have entered the capital. But the war definitely isn't quite over yet. The Greeks have been phenomenal, anyway, you have to give them that, keeping up the fight ever since 28 October last year.

3 MAY

War between Iraq and Britain! The Iraqi regime has implored Hitler for help. Arabia may be on the move. What a ghastly prospect!

The Greek campaign is over. The British have completed another successful 'embarkation' (that's *one* thing they're good at). I assume the king and government have retreated to Crete.

13 MAY

Today's huge sensation – Rudolf Hess, Hitler's deputy, flew to the British Isles in a Messerschmitt plane and parachuted safely to the ground, where a Scottish farm-worker looked after him and took him to hospital in Glasgow. Now we've seen everything! It happened on Saturday night. Though the world was left in ignorance of it until now. The German papers initially assumed it was a fatal accident and wrote obituaries for him. Word that he had landed in Scotland came as a shock to the German people. The official party line is that severe physical pain had left him prey to 'delusions'. One passage from Berlin claimed that he 'imagined that by personal sacrifice he could forestall a development which in his eyes would end with the complete crushing of the British empire'. Hee hee! Rudolf Hess looks more honourable and wholesome than the other party bigwigs – and perhaps this step shows that he *is* more honourable. The whole world is extremely curious at the moment to know what prompted his flight.

22 MAY

It was Karin's seventh birthday yesterday. I wrote in my diary on this day last year: 'God grant that the world will look different by Karin's next birthday!' And it certainly does look different, but there's no sign of any changes for the better. Possibly Sweden and the other Nordic countries are in slightly less danger, the main focus now seems to be on the Mediterranean, North Africa and the Middle East. Yesterday the Germans launched an air invasion on Crete, or was it the day before? What's left of Greek resistance is concentrated there, with British assistance.

Just like last year, summer arrived on Karin's birthday. It was the first day you could go out without a coat. But everything's much, much later this year – I don't think I've ever known such a cold spring. Today, though, was really *warm* and you could really see everything turning green all of a sudden. Karin, Sture and I went out to Judarn and it was lovely; Lars went to the scouts' elk-horn festival.

For her birthday yesterday, Karin got her first bike and various other goodies such as dolls' shoes, books, plasticine, coloured crayons, woollen gloves, money, chocolate and so on. Elsa-Lena, Matte, Anders and their mothers were here. Then we parents celebrated the birthday with a visit to Dramaten [theatre] (while the birthday girl was sleeping) with Gullanders and Viridéns, followed by supper in the back restaurant at the Strand [hotel].

Tomorrow we'll put Karin and Matte's names down for school. Though Karin can already read pretty well. She's learning to swim and ride a bike now, too.

Well, we'll have to see how things look by Karin's next birthday, and whether we have peace or not. It's not worth getting one's hopes up.

25 MAY

Today is Mother's Day and yesterday – according to Sture – was Mother's Eve. That was why I found myself getting an early present of a fine pair of silk stockings, a book, *Mrs Miniver,* and a box of chocolates, plus two pink roses (though I had to buy those myself) and a 'picsher' from Karin: 'To Mother'. And today Sture and Karin went out to buy a cake covered in green marzipan. Lars spent last night and the early hours of this morning in a bunker on Kungsholmen, summoned there as a scout 'in accordance with Emergency Legislation §10,' I think that was it. They must be doing air-raid exercises. It's been a lovely warm day, and Karin, Sture and I went out to Djurgården very early and left the flat in quite a state. Lars was supposed to get himself cleaned up while we were out but was still filthy when we got back and had to be chased back into the bathroom.

Djurgården was lovely with all its pale-green leaves, but when I got back I promised myself never to go out and leave the place that untidy again.

In the afternoon I went out towards Karlberg with the kids, i.e. Karin rode her bike and Lars held on. After a couple of hours in the heat we were pretty irritable and the children argued and I was cross with Lars, who treated Karin very loutishly.

Then we had hash for dinner in high good humour, followed by cake; I washed up and Karin came round selling plasticine sweets. Then it was Karin's bedtime and I read her some of *A Little Princess*. Lars read Albert Engström. Now both children are in bed, Sture's at his desk reading Albert Engström and I'm on the sofa beside my pink roses, writing this.

See how peacefully we live in Stockholm in 1941, while the rest of the world looks wretched. The battlecruiser *Hood*, the world's largest warship, was sunk off Greenland by the German battleship *Bismarck*. It had a crew of 1,300 men, of whom very few were saved. Thirteen hundred souls less in the world, in the blinking of an eye!

There's trouble in Crete. Germany has apparently occupied the western section of the island. If the Germans really do manage to conquer Crete by invading from the air, there's a risk that Britain will finally experience the long-anticipated invasion attempt on its own island.

They're imposing a tax on luxury goods here soon!

28 MAY

And then the *Bismarck* was sunk in its turn, by a British battlecruiser torpedo. I saw on a newspaper billboard that there were 3,000 men on board. That may be an overestimate, but probably not by much. The loss of the *Bismarck* must mean more to the German navy than the *Hood* to the British.

According to the headlines in the evening papers, the British have now abandoned their resistance in Crete.

Roosevelt gave a 'fireside chat' yesterday and proclaimed a national state of emergency in the USA.

I JUNE

Iraq has asked for a ceasefire. The British are the victors there, for a change. But they've definitely run out of fight on Crete.

8 JUNE

Today the British anticipated the Germans for once, by marching into Syria, which is apparently today's battleground. De Gaulle's French forces are fighting alongside the British.

At work today there were lots of worrying rumours from Gotland. German troop ships skirted the west coast of the island and this clearly made everyone feel extremely nervous. A lot of the soldiers wrote formal goodbyes to their loved ones.

Kaiser Wilhelm died the other day and will be buried in Dutch soil. So he, one of the leading figures in the last war, didn't get to see the end of this one.

16 JUNE

Our old king is 84 today. May he outlive this war.

I'm in such a melancholy and anxious mood tonight. Again it's one of those warm, rain-dampened summer evenings I recall from the eventful days of last summer. And things seem to be happening now. Relations between Germany and Russia are at a critical point. It says in the evening papers that there's general mobilization in Russia. Germany's had significant forces stationed on its eastern border for a long time, of course, and this past week it's been transporting its men to Finland in large numbers. They were the ones who passed close to Gotland and made everyone so uneasy there. If it comes to war between Germany and Finland on one side and Russia on the other, we'll be in a terrible situation. The question is whether we'll have any chance of staying out of it. The Germans no doubt want Gotland as an airbase.

Today I got everything ready for the trip to Furusund. On Saturday I finished work for the summer after a pleasant farewell lunch at Pilen with Hamberg, Bågstam, Flory, Anne-Marie, schoolmaster Kjellberg and someone I didn't know. This evening A.M. came round, worried, and I'm worried, too. Kock and several of the other officers are leaving their posts.

Karin and Matte finished their swimming lessons at the Palace of Sport today. And Karin can ride her bike. All would be sweetness and light, if it weren't for the anxiety. Sture maintains that Germany and Britain will join forces against Russia, and that this was Hess's peace plan. But that's just too fantastical to be true.

22 JUNE

This morning at half-past four, German troops crossed the Russian border from both Romania and Germany, and perhaps in other places too. So now it's war between the former allies, and poor Finland's in the firing line again. Germany claims Russia has totally failed to stick to its treaty with Germany and has in fact done all it can to injure Germany, and Russia claims the opposite and says Germany attacked without provocation. Vast numbers of troops are now ranged against one another on either sides of borders from the Arctic Ocean in the north to the Black Sea in the south.

The future is one big question mark. How will things go for Sweden? All leave has been cancelled over midsummer. In the shipping lanes off Furusund, several steamers have just had to sit there waiting and some have turned back, presumably because they couldn't get through to their destinations. Large parts of the Baltic have been mined by the Germans.

It's been a hot summer's day with brilliant sunshine. Sture came out from town on a packed ferry and hadn't heard a thing about any war because he'd been on the boat since 8 o'clock. But everyone's very worried. Only Grandmother has stayed calm, and says, 'It'll all be over soon.' But I think that, on the contrary, it's just started. The really strange thing is that one has to back Germany now. It would be too awkward, of course, to side with Germany against Russia and with Britain against Germany. It's all such a mess. We can hear the booming of heavy guns on this radio we've just borrowed. Oh yes, and Italy's also declared that it considers itself at war with the Soviet Union.

28 JUNE

I ought to paste in Hitler's speech on the outbreak of war here, but I'll have to do it at the end instead. I'm sitting in bed, looking out on the fine drizzle over the sea, after an unsettled night doing battle with mosquitoes, with the *thunder of guns* in the distance. At any rate, the ladies' defence volunteers in Copenhagen claim that's what we can hear, from the Åland Sea.

Since I last wrote, the Swedish government has granted permission for *one German division* from the north of Norway to travel through Sweden to Finland, which in other words means we'll let through any number of them. We've no other option, of course. Once more, it's Finland that is at stake. The Russians are bombing in Finland again – Åbo [Turku], for example, has taken a terrible pounding, and Åbo Castle has suffered major damage. Hungary has declared itself at war with Russia.

The Germans are providing no information about how far they've got in Russia – and the reason is said to be that Russia's lines of communication are in disarray, so the Germans don't want to reveal their position.

The Baltic states are busy liberating themselves – at any rate, I think the Russians are gone from Lithuania.

National Socialism and Bolshevism – it's rather like two giant reptiles doing battle. It's not pleasant having to side with either reptile, but for now one can only wish the Soviet Union will get well and truly thrashed, given all that they've grabbed for themselves in the course of this war and all the harm it has done to Finland. In Britain and America they now have to side with Bolshevism, which must be even harder and I'm sure the man in the street finds it hard to keep up with it all. Queen Wilhelmina of Holland said on the radio that she was prepared to support Russia but with one reservation: that she still disapproved of the principles of Bolshevism.

The biggest bodies of troops in world history are massed against each other on the eastern front. It's appalling to think of. Is Armageddon looming?

I've been working my way through some general history here in Furusund and it makes for dreadfully depressing reading – war and war and war and suffering for humanity. And they *never* learn but just carry on drenching the planet in blood, sweat and tears.

2 JULY

Since my last entry, the Germans have made good progress. Russian forces of 300–400,000 have been encircled at Białystok and are facing certain death, Libau [Liepāja] and Riga have been taken, according to today's *Aftonbladet* Murmansk has fallen, etc., etc. There's been an appalling amount of bloodshed. Lemberg [Lviv] has fallen. There was fighting there during the First World War, too, I remember.

13 JULY

The Stalin Line has been broken. It runs in the area of Daugava, Dnieper and Dniester. That's not particularly far from Moscow.

What's more, America occupied Iceland a little while back. And French resistance in Syria, which seems to have been more formal, has been broken and a local ceasefire has been brokered between the British and French. I think that's all the important news since I last wrote.

But it's clear that things are grim on the eastern front. As the Russians retreat, they are to evacuate the country on Stalin's orders, which means they have to remove the civilian population. And I bet that's not being done with kid gloves. It's a relief that I lack the imagination to visualize all the suffering.

19 AUGUST

I've been completely neglecting my diary. I hardly know what has been going on, only that things are very tense between the USA and Japan, so a declaration of war can be expected at any moment; that the war continues in Russia but perhaps not at quite the same pace as before, although the Finns have retaken large areas round Lake Ladoga and the Germans have also pushed far into the country; that Roosevelt and Churchill met in the middle of the Atlantic and released a joint declaration of their views on peace, that US aid to Britain has been increasing bit by bit; that – according to information in today's reports – the Germans don't believe in ultimate victory (and Russia will prove hard-boiled), that the British are bombing for all they are worth, and, well, that's all I can remember for now.

Tomorrow the war will be two years old. To me it feels as if it's been going on for ever.

> *[Press cutting of a picture of Churchill in profile with cap and cigar, with Astrid's handwritten caption: 'Hitler's No. 1 Enemy!' Press cutting from* Dagens Nyheter, *31 August 1941: 'Two years of war'.]*

The Finns have retaken Vyborg [Viipuri] – it must be an emotional moment for every Finn. The Finnish flag is flying from Vyborg Castle again – even though it had to be hastily made out of a bed sheet. The Finns will probably soon have taken back everything they lost in the peace settlement of 13 March 1940, and then I hope they'll stop and let Germany deal with the rest.

It will hardly be a popular birthday to celebrate. Here's a voice from the depths of the ordinary people:

> *[Typed transcript of a letter Astrid saw in her work at the censor's office, a rather erratically written and misspelt outpouring, a personal view of the warring sides and the progress of the war in Swedish.]*

Oh, and I forgot to write that Britain and Russia have occupied Iran and forced it into submission.

6 SEPTEMBER

*[Press cutting from Dagens Nyheter, 6 September 1941:
'Quisling attacks Swedish opinion', reporting a Quisling
speech in which he accuses the Swedish press of repeatedly
publishing untrue propaganda critical of the 'new Norway'.]*

It's enough to make you choke! I hope he dies alone! I'm glad to hear he's apparently suffering from insomnia and accidentally took an almost fatal dose of sleeping tablets the other night.

Germany on the rampage all over Europe. O Lord, for how long? And they take all the food, wherever they go. Like a plague of locusts in Egypt. The following three cuttings from the daily papers are all from the same day (7 September 1941):

*[Press cutting from Dagens Nyheter: 'Germans execute
French hostages': three Frenchmen held in reprisal after an
attack on a French soldier in Paris are put to death. Press
cutting from Dagens Nyheter: 'All Jews in Germany forced
to wear yellow star'. Press cutting from Stockholms-
Tidningen: 'All Norway without radio', radio sets confiscated
from all except members of the National Unity Party.]*

II SEPTEMBER

A state of emergency was declared in Oslo yesterday. At the first special court [of summary justice], two people were executed by firing squad, one received a life sentence, two got fifteen years and another got ten. Those executed were a leader of the trade union confederation, lawyer Viggo Hansteen, and union chairman Rolf Wickstrøm. And this in a

Nordic country! It makes your heart feel like bursting in your breast with impotent rage and despair.

No one is allowed out after 8 in the evening. God, how they'll hate it in Norway!

Quisling's latest speech apparently caused outrage in Norway and a general strike was planned in Oslo. The official response was to impose a state of emergency.

And in Russia they're at it hammer and tongs. The youth of Finland is bleeding to death on the battlefields. Several people I know of through work have fallen, among them Väinö Tanner's only son, who was engaged to a Swedish girl. Leningrad's communication lines to the rest of Russia are severed. There are rumours of a separate peace between Russia and Finland on the basis of the old borders.

I OCTOBER

Things have happened [in English] since I last wrote.

On 17 September the Swedish navy suffered a terrible disaster in Hårsfjärden [fjord]. For reasons as yet unexplained, the destroyer *Göteborg* exploded and sank, taking two other destroyers down with it, the *Klas Horn* and the *Klas Uggla*. There was burning oil all over the surface of the water where the poor crew were trying to save themselves. Thirty-three men died (as luck would have it, most were on shore leave). According to our letters, the aftermath was an appalling sight to behold. Arms, legs and severed heads were strewn everywhere and salvage teams were going round with sticks, hooking down tattered flesh and guts from the branches of the trees. One of them describes finding one of his best friends, his face untouched but the rest of him horribly mangled, another wrote of standing on the jetty, about to light a cigarette when a human arm suddenly hit him in the face. There's speculation that it was caused by negligence when they were demonstrating a new torpedo but we have five accounts that all swear they saw a bomb fall from one of the planes circling over Hårsfjärden. If they're right, it was all caused by an accidental bomb drop. The idea of sabotage also suggests itself – particularly as we read in the papers today that another gang of saboteurs, who favoured explosives, have been arrested.

Further reports from the domestic front say that there's a shortage of eggs now. I'm glad of my 20kg of preserved eggs, because we only get 7 eggs per person per month.

In Norway the special court was dissolved after a few days, but now they've introduced it in Czechoslovakia and the death penalties are coming thick and fast. The Norwegians have been told to hand over their blankets to the German fighting forces, or there'll be hell to pay. All the occupied countries have to give their entire food stock to Germany but even so the people are starving there, too, like the rest of Europe. The food situation in France is intolerable, and it's the same in Finland and Norway.

The Finns have taken Petrozavodsk, the evening papers say. The Murmansk railway line has been entirely cut. But I'm sure there won't be any resolution in Russia in time for the winter.

And we've moved from 12 Vulcanusgatan to 46 Dalagatan, despite the war and the high prices. I can't help feeling pleased about our new flat, though I'm always aware that we've done nothing to deserve our good fortune, when there are so many without a roof over their heads.

My 1940 pocket diary went astray in the move.

We now have a lovely big living room, the children each have their own room and then there's our bedroom. We've bought quite a lot of new furniture and made it look really nice; I really don't want it to get bombed.

The Germans are about 150km from Moscow, apparently, and 170 Russian divisions are said to be surrounded. It's hard to know what's true and what's not.

Tomorrow is the last day we'll be able to enjoy Danish pastries and other butter-enriched dough products. Oh, I don't think I made a note here about the egg ration, which was set a while ago at 7–8 eggs per person per month. Luckily I've got a good number preserved, but they are for another year, if the war lasts!

My darling daughter starts school this autumn. I'm having a few problems with her at the moment: she's hostile and disobedient and always showing off. I *do hope* it's just a phase.

The battle goes on and the world endures optimum suffering. Nothing but devilry and hooliganism wherever you look. Reading the paper yesterday evening I was plunged into depression by the woeful state of the world. Britain's considering a declaration of war on Finland because Finland won't make a separate peace with Russia, and the USA is urging Finland in the same direction. The USA tried to mediate an agreement between Finland and Russia back in August, but Finland refused.

The Germans are now about 40km from Moscow, which is to be defended 'to the death'. Today's story: Stalin sends a telegram to Hitler, 'If these irritating border incidents don't stop, then I shall mobilize.' There's something in that. It's true that the Germans have penetrated far into the country but great, sacred Russia is still not that easy to mobilize. There's an article in *Dagens Nyheter* today about the winter war, which appears scarcely avoidable, though the Germans must have been pretty sure Russia would be on its knees before winter arrived. Just reading the article froze me to the bone, given the appalling difficulty of fighting such a war. The Germans have taken the Crimea, evidently suffering enormous losses.

Other things that have happened recently include the following:

The Germans sank an American destroyer, part of a convoy, which was admittedly not taken lightly by Roosevelt, but was still not considered sufficient provocation for war.

And Europe is starving. Athens has nothing to eat, the paper said yesterday, and in France they are surviving on vegetables as best they can. In Germany things are far worse, even though they grab everything they can, and in Helsinki the police had to break up the crowds queuing to buy herring.

Those German ruffians are still running amok; the Norwegians have had to give them blankets, ski boots, anoraks, tents, skis, radio sets and almost all their food and (according to Aina Molin) their latest demand – bedclothes. The Jews of Berlin are being forcibly transported to Poland in massive numbers, and one can imagine what that means. They're accommodated in ghettos surrounded by barbed-wire fences and are now shot without warning if they try to venture outside their enclosure. Their food rations are no more than half what other people get.

The other day there was a sign in some kind of bookshop on Beridarebansgatan [in Stockholm]: 'No admittance to Jews and half-Jews.' A crowd gathered outside and there was a terrible fuss; now the ÖÄ [the over-governor, the highest city official] has ordered the owner to put the sign where it can't be seen from the street.

Talking of *Gräuel* [atrocity propaganda], one hears awful accounts of Russian rampages in the Baltic states before they had to retreat in the face of German advances. Nails driven through babies' tongues while their mothers looked on, and other such horrors one almost refuses to believe, but they're very likely true. Human sadism seems capable of going to any lengths. Thousands upon thousands are missing, hauled off to Siberia or killed.

Misery knows no borders, it seems, and there's no end in sight.

6 DECEMBER

Independence Day in Finland brought a declaration of war from Britain. We live in a strange world and no mistake: in winter 1939, Britain asked Sweden to let British troops through to aid Finland against Russia, which was secretly being helped by Germany to suppress that troublesome little band, the Finnish people. But the Russians have suddenly assumed such great, sacred and heroic proportions in British eyes that it's now 'Shame on you, Finland!' for going on the attack. And former allies Germany and Russia are at daggers drawn. Things change fast. Yet the only possible state of affairs is that both the British and the Americans understand Finland with heart and soul, though they have to say otherwise. And I read in a newspaper somewhere that the Poles and Russians have agreed to 'let bygones by bygones'. That seems to me a rather cute way of describing many centuries of hostility and 100 years of oppression on the Russians' part. But hatred of Germany can evidently achieve wonders.

Oh, I forgot to mention – Hangö [Hanko], bone of contention since the 1939 negotiations between Russia and Finland – is again in Finnish hands.

8 DECEMBER

WORLD WAR no. 2 is now a fact. Japan opened hostilities on the United States yesterday by repeatedly bombing Pearl Harbor on Hawaii, and Manila. Later, a statement was read on the radio in Tokyo that from dawn on Monday morning a state of war existed in the Pacific between Japan on one side and the United States and Britain on the other.

Japan has attacked Thailand, which immediately capitulated in the face of the threat to bomb Bangkok.

Now all we are waiting for is America's declaration of war on Germany. Then the Axis Powers will be united against the democracies – one gigantic battle spanning the globe.

We currently have fighting in the Russian forests, the Libyan desert and on sunny Hawaii. And it all started because the Germans wanted Danzig. It makes one feel quite light-headed to think about it.

The fact is that things aren't all going the Germans' way in Russia. The war that was meant to be over long before winter arrived is carrying on as if nothing's happened. In the Moscow area things are moving forward for the Germans, though slowly, whereas on the southern front they were forced to pull back, with major losses. You don't break mighty Russia just like that. There'll surely be no Christmas leave for German soldiers this year. Pity the poor little soldiers all around the world!

And King Leopold, who has been a widower since that tragic day in August 1935 when Queen Astrid died in the car crash, has remarried.

11 DECEMBER

The Japanese have sunk two big British battleships, the *Repulse* and the *Prince of Wales*, the morning papers reported. In the Pacific. Huge outcry in Britain. They think the Japanese have death pilots willing to sacrifice their lives to pull off a grand coup for their [Britain's] enemy.

This afternoon there was an even bigger sensation. The Axis has declared war on the USA. It was expected, of course, but even so it feels rather ghastly that the whole globe has now been drawn into the tangle. For us here in Sweden it will mean all communication with the USA is cut off: post and so on has all been going via Germany.

And China has declared war on Germany.

At work today I also saw some awful pictures of Finnish children who had been carried off to Russia and had now come back. I haven't seen anything as horrifically emaciated and deformed since the days of the World War, sorry, I mean the *First* World War. But this is how all the children of Europe will look by the end of it all.

26 DECEMBER

Since I last wrote, something remarkable has happened: von Brauchitsch, supreme commander of the German army, has stepped down and been succeeded by Hitler himself. There's much speculation as to why. Perhaps it takes the Führer's personal intervention to energize the troops in Russia, where things are going badly for Germany and the wretched soldiers have to live in dugouts in minus 40°. The November offensive against Moscow has to be seen as an error of judgement; the general belief is that Hitler himself ordered it, going against von Brauchitsch's opinion, and that B. has now been made a scapegoat. Be that as it may, this development is interpreted as a sign of weakness.

The war has continued unabated over Christmas; the Japanese are raising merry hell in the Pacific, Hong Kong has fallen, Manila is very vulnerable, etc., etc.

At Näs we celebrated Christmas in the usual manner with loads of food, and some splendidly seasonal weather, starting on Christmas Eve (we'd had a snowless winter until then) with a heavy fall of snow, which made all the trees and bushes look like a Christmas card for the day itself. Today, the 26th, it's minus 10.

The predominant feeling here in Sweden as Christmas approached was naturally a profound and fervent gratitude that we can still mark it as we do.

(Though we've had to settle for ten Christmas tree candles per child this year.)

1942

Astrid, 1942. From the
Svenska Dagbladet *archive.*

A new year begins. I wonder what the three gentlemen opposite are expecting from the New Year. Hitler, at any rate, looks as if he's had a few sleepless nights. Churchill looks sad and troubled; only Roosevelt looks hopeful, in that American way. But maybe the photo was taken before the Japanese attacked.

[Newspaper pictures of Roosevelt,
Churchill and Hitler pasted in.]

Things aren't looking all that bright for Germany, in fact. They can't conceal how badly things have been going in Russia for quite some time now! When all is said and done, we can only give a sigh and hope: please let Germany keep Russia in check! Because what will happen otherwise?

How will things look, when this is all over? Still no sign of the peace that all humanity is longing for. How many souls will be despatched 'to death and deadly night' before deliverance arrives?

In Norway, 11 of its nationals were executed by firing squad a few days ago. Sheer instinct for self-preservation makes it hard not to wish Germany defeat!

[Short press cutting: account of 1 February 1942 by
Gunnar Cederschiöld of Stockholms-Tidningen *on the*
privations being suffered by the people of Athens.]

This is Greece today, according to *Stockholms-Tidningen*'s correspondent. And it isn't that much better anywhere in Europe except here in Sweden. France will have to approach Germany, I read in one of the papers the other day; they can't bear the food shortage and misery any longer. In Belgium people are fainting from hunger on the street, in Finland and Norway things are wretched and of course in Germany too. I don't know what it's like in Russia, but it doesn't take much imagination to guess.

And we're having yet another dreadfully cold winter. People will freeze and come to harm, it's enough to make you weep.

At a formal ceremony at Akershus [Fortress] on Sunday afternoon, Reich Commissar Terboven announced that Quisling is to be prime minister of Norway.

Since I last wrote there have been major developments, which I should have entered in here far more regularly. One of them is that *Singapore* has fallen, which happens – it's said – only once a century. I'd saved a cutting about what happened, but seem to have mislaid it. The Japanese show of strength in the Pacific is exceptional. To think that Singapore, a fortress Britain has used for maintaining a key position for centuries, could be taken by the Japanese after so short a time – it says a lot about the abilities of the Japanese and maybe even more about the appalling nonchalance of the British. It led to a governmental crisis in Britain, but Churchill managed to ride out the storm as usual. There was even more consternation about a week ago (I think it was the 13th or 14th) when two German battleships, the *Scharnhorst* and the *Gneisenau*, put to sea in broad daylight from Brest, where they had been subjected to intensive bombing for months, and made it back home to the North Sea without the British lifting a finger. To go back to the Pacific, where the most important events are currently being played out, attacks are expected imminently on Sumatra, Java, India and the Burma Road, and Australia, where all men fit for military service have been called up for defence duties. I simply can't *fathom* what Britain and America are playing at – the Japanese are carrying on like monsters. They say things have been appalling, these past few weeks in Singapore. The fortress could only be defended on the seaward side, it seems, and the Japanese came stealing across the Malay peninsula, where there seem to have been scarcely any defensive measures. Lack of water was 'the last drop, which made the cup run over' (a fine way of putting it). Women and children were evacuated over to Sumatra as the bombs rained down. The British had scarcely any aircraft in Singapore; how is something like that even possible?

In Russia, '37,000 men' have been mown down, all told.

Finland's fronts are holding nice and firm.

Here in Sweden there have been a lot of call-ups in recent days. Foreign Minister Günther said in a briefing yesterday that our position, though serious, hasn't got any worse, but the country needs to strengthen its defences now spring is coming. I daresay they're expecting a British attack on Norway. But there's still no sign of spring. Here in Stockholm it's been below zero since 5 January; the whole Baltic's packed with ice, Gotland's cut off – it's a simply diabolical winter – the third in a row – and a total torment. Personally I can't remember a longer winter but I expect that's because of the cough Karin's had – it started four months ago today and at the moment she's in my bed, just the same as she was then, with a cough, a runny nose and a temperature. We took her for an X-ray: it showed a now-healed inflammation of the left lung, and the cardiogram showed that the inflammation has affected the heart muscles; there's a murmur. Ottander says he thinks it will gradually pass, *but what if it doesn't?* I'm so tired of, so anxious about, her wretched cough and poor health generally that it's currently worrying me more than the whole world war.

16 MARCH

Karin's been to the doctor's and she's almost better now, and the heart murmur is much improved. But she had a few pus cells in her urine, which will be treated with some kind of sulphonamide preparation.

I don't think I wrote about Java capitulating, in the course of which 98,000 Dutch and British were taken prisoner. The Dutch empire no longer exists – and what about its British counterpart? Australia is expecting an attack.

In Riom, they're holding trials of those responsible for the destruction of France.

The situation has been critical here in Sweden and possibly still is. We've had evacuation instructions – and yet we seem to be taking everything relatively calmly, compared to the start of the war, when we simply couldn't stop talking about the evacuation when we met at the park.

Seventeen [Norwegian] newspapers were impounded yesterday for a report on conditions in Norwegian prisons. If it's true – and there's no reason to doubt it – then it's so shockingly horrific that it makes you feel sick to read about it. Pure sadism and medieval torture. Malnutrition is becoming widespread among the Norwegian people.

Here in Sweden there's still food, but we're definitely starting to feel the pinch. We're getting less and less meat – and come the summer I expect our ration will be pretty limited. I haven't the stamina to write about all this misery.

GOOD FRIDAY

The snow's back after a couple of days of fine weather and dry streets. I don't think spring will ever come this year – after the coldest winter since meteorological records began.

Under cover of the blizzard, the 11 Norwegian ships that have been in the port of Göteborg since the Germans occupied Norway tried to make for the British Isles. The Swedish government had impounded them until it was clear who the rightful owners were. Germany laid claim to them, of course, but didn't get them – following the Supreme Court ruling the other day. Every Norwegian in Sweden, or so it seemed, saw a chance to escape to Britain. But the Germans were waiting like beasts of prey just outside Swedish territorial waters and three ships were set on fire, two returned to Göteborg and six were apparently chased out to sea. In our letters we've had so many accounts of the Norwegians who thought they would try their luck this way that the sinking of these ships feels particularly ghastly, just because the whole enterprise was so foolhardy from the start. Those on board must have had to accept that the voyage could be their last.

And here I sit in my home that's all spick and span for Easter, as if there were nothing bad or evil in the world. Tomorrow I shall have been married 11 years. Karin's caught another cold, which I hope is now on the way out. It's our first Easter in our new home on Dalagatan and Karin's pleased that there will be so many places to hide the eggs, i.e., the children's chocolate eggs. Scarcely a soul has any real eggs in this town, but I was able to borrow 12 from Anne-Marie, who gets an extra allocation because Stellan's ill.

To go back to world politics, things seem to be stagnating a bit for the Japanese in the Pacific. There's been no sign of any invasion of Australia. I don't really know what's going on in Russia; I suppose the German spring offensive won't be getting under way just yet.

19 APRIL

The Americans have bombed Tokyo, which has been a cause for great rejoicing in the USA. I scarcely know what's happening in the world nowadays, but Russia's presumably still fighting at full throttle, to judge by the news we hear of numbers dead and exterminated.

Laval has come back into the French government; he seems to be some sort of Quisling, supposed to bring France closer to Germany.

The British are engaged in heavy bombing of Germany.

In Stockholm yesterday we had the highest April temperatures since 1880, according to the records: 23°. And a fortnight ago it was snowing heavily. Now it's nice and dry everywhere, the sun's shining and it's warm, as I said. But I expect it will turn cold again. Today all four of us were out at Haga Park in the morning. Then Karin and I went to the pictures and saw a Marx Brothers film. Sture's living for the exhibition (Motormännen 42) that M. is putting on. Lars went off for a walk in the suit he's slightly grown out of. He'll be getting a new one at confirmation time. That'll use up masses of coupons.

We'll definitely have very restricted amounts of meat by the summer. The occasional egg has at last started to pop up from time to time. Butter seems scarce to me, but it may well get worse.

The king had an operation for bladder stones, I don't know if I wrote about that before, and came through it well, which we were all glad to hear.

In Norway there's great discord among the clergy and Bishop Berggrav was almost sent to a concentration camp in Germany, but for some reason it didn't happen.

I'm reading Remarque's refugee book *Liebe Deinen Nächsten* [*Love Thy Neighbour*, published in English as *Flotsam*], which describes the Via Dolorosa of all the Jewish emigrants. It's appalling, and from what I see at work I can confirm the truth of it.

All round Europe people are keeling over in the street and dying of starvation – things are probably worst in Greece – but it's frightful in France and Belgium too.

12 MAY

Since I last wrote, Hitler has made a speech, which I should paste in here, but it was so long I can't be bothered. The speech was remarkable, however, for seeming to hint at internal divisions in Germany, because Hitler requested – and got – exceptional powers to add to those he already had – to stamp out war fatigue in whatever form it showed itself and to remove from office all individuals not rising to the demands of the hour. 'The demands of the hour' must be rather difficult for Germany at the moment – that was the main impression one got from the speech – and at work we immediately noticed obvious despondency about Germany's ability to win. The speech has resulted in a similar reaction in various parts of the world, in fact. Faith in German victory is pretty minimal.

I wrote about Hitler's speech first, just because it ought to come in chronological order; but in fact there's a hideously more important thing that should have come first under this day's date – today, for the first time in this war, we've heard reports of the use of *GAS* – and it wouldn't surprise me if this is the prelude to an even nastier phase of this nasty war. I wrote once during the Finnish winter war that the Russians had used gas – but then no more was heard of it, so perhaps it wasn't true. Now, though, the Germans have started using some kind of nerve gas down in the Crimea, which caught the Russian soldiers unawares. According to *Aftonbladet*, this nerve gas isn't fatal but just stuns its targets so they can be taken captive. But once it's started, you can be sure that in no time they'll start using the most horrendous of gases. We started to think something was up when Churchill made a speech the other day, warning the Germans against using gas; because if they did, Britain would retaliate by hurling huge amounts of the stuff down on Germany. German preparations for the gas war naturally couldn't be kept secret. Of course it's surprising in a way that the Germans didn't heed the warning when they must realize the implications for their own people of a gas war with no holds barred. But then humanity has simply and irredeemably taken leave of its senses. There they all are, Britain, America, Russia and Germany, hollering about the ghastliest lethal gases they've got stocks of – as if that were anything to boast about, when they actually agreed from the outset not to use gas. (Ha, ha!) And of course it's evident that Germany sees its own situation as precarious, if it has to resort to weapons of that kind to bring things to a head on the eastern front.

Plenty of other things have happened since last time. The prime minister of Denmark, Stauning, has died. He was the one who in a speech in Lund long ago argued against the idea of a Nordic defence union. It would be entertaining to know how things would actually look up here in the north at the moment, if such a union had been set up in the years before the war. Maybe the whole region would be untouched now!

Also, the British have occupied Madagascar despite French opposition. Laval is taking France closer to the Axis Powers, which is causing serious complications for its relations with Britain and the USA.

And Hitler and Musso had another little meeting – I expect it was to agree to start the gassing again. Any encounter between those two generally has some immediate and fiendish outcome.

Today's official reports contained distressing news about the food situation in Finland. It seems they've neither enough cereal seed nor enough seed potatoes to plant. So how will they cope next winter? If things get any worse than they are already, the lot of them will starve to death. Gunnar went over there to organize agricultural assistance from here in Sweden, but what use is extra labour if there's nothing to sow or plant? Poor, poor Finns – our streets are full of disabled Finnish soldiers, some of whom look not much older than Lars, hopping on one leg or with only one arm…

Apart from that, we're waiting for rain. If Our Lord doesn't take mercy on us and let us have a good harvest this year, there'll be hunger here, too – that's definite. It's already getting quite hard to devise meals – even if things are grand for us, compared to other people.

Recent reports have included some lavish words of praise from foreigners for us, the hitherto much-decried Swedes. We were said to be 'a nation of Samaritans', among other things. And I think it's true that we are helping as best we can.

The Germans have carried out numerous executions by firing squad in the occupied countries recently – 18 young Norwegians, 72 Dutch, a lot of French, all for assaults on Germans. But how can there be anything else but assaults when they make themselves so hated everywhere?

Well, that's how the world looks in this year of grace 1942, and a confoundedly cold and unpleasant year it's been, too. The day after tomorrow on Ascension Day, Lars and Göran are getting confirmed. Can't there be an end to the war soon, please *can't* there? What sort of future will there be otherwise for those who are young and on the threshold of the world? How hard it will be to inherit a bloody, hideous wasteland of a world, gassed and wretched in every way.

21 MAY

The gas turned out to be a hoax. The reporter responsible for the story was ordered to leave Berlin at once. So far there's no gas war then, at any rate.

Karin turned eight today. In previous years it's always been summer and warm but this year we've had *rain*, to our indescribable delight; today it's dry, but cold and raw. Karin's presents comprised Lasse's old watch ('Just think, it still works,' Linnéa overheard her whispering, enraptured, on the way to school), a suitcase, a purse, two books, a box of chocolates, flowers, a total of 12 kronor from various people, several bookmarks and a slate. Matte and Elsa-Lena came round with their mothers, and Karin Bené was here too.

The mums talked coupons and food, as they always do these days, and Elsa, who recently had a visit from an undernourished Greta Wikberg from Finland, told us what's on the menu in a well-to-do Helsinki home nowadays. In the morning rye-flour porridge without bread or milk, for lunch rye-flour porridge with a piece of bread and 1dl milk, for dinner boiled frozen potatoes with grated swede, for which one has queued for hours, with possibly a little thin fruit soup to follow, then in the evening lingonberry-leaf tea and a bit of bread, and that's it. Why, our rations are pure gluttony, though we think them stingy.

Oh, and Lars was confirmed on 14 May in Adolf Fredrik Church along with 43 other lads. Afterwards we had a 'reception' with wine, coffee, cake and biscuits. Elsa, Alli, Lecka, Pelle Viridén and Matte, Elsa-Lena and Peter here.

We gave Lars a watch and he had cufflinks from Lecka and a four-colour pen from Elsa and Alli – and some flowers besides. Then we had a family dinner of smörgåsbord, guinea fowl and cake. We certainly are well off in this land of Sweden.

[Typed transcript of a letter from Holland, from Astrid's work at the censor's office.]

5 JULY

Since last time, plenty's happened that I've neglected to write about. The main focus of interest has been the Desert War. Rommel's been storming ahead and is now a good way into Egypt, threatening Alexandria and Cairo. These past few days we've been constantly expecting to hear that Alexandria's fallen into German hands, but just for the moment there seems to be a short-lived pause. Tobruk, which has been fought over avidly, fell a short time ago, and in the process many British soldiers were taken captive by the Germans. The Italians seem to have joined in the fighting for once. Rommel's so skilful that the *British* have virtually made him a national hero for having routed the Eighth Army.

To think that it's now over a year since the Germans marched on Russia. It would all be over and done with before the winter, they said, but instead the German army got frozen in and had to endure terrible hardships. As for the big spring offensive they kept bragging about, there's been no sign of it, even if the Germans have made some advances and awful, bloody battles have been raging in the Crimea, where Sebastopol recently fell.

A Swedish steamship, the *Ada Gorthon*, was torpedoed in *Swedish* waters by a Russian submarine and another had a Russian torpedo fired at it, off Västervik.

Sweden seems to be producing a good harvest, thank God, because there would have been famine otherwise. We've had so much rain and it's been dreadfully cold. I had my first outdoor swim yesterday, 4 July, down by the boatyard. I was in Vimmerby for three weeks but it was no good for swimming, too cold and windy. Now I'm in Furusund with Sture, Karin and Gunvor and hope we can get down to bathing in earnest. Karin's so well now – at last – after her persistent winter cough. Lars has stayed on at Näs and is trying his hand at farming. He and I had a nice four-day cycling trip: Vimmerby – Horn – Kisa – Norra Vi – Tranås – Skurugata – Eksjö – Hult – Bällö [now Bellö] – Kråkshult – Vimmerby. How beautiful Småland is.

We're not getting any coal from Germany and are finding it terribly hard to produce any wood domestically, so the fuel situation for the winter looks pretty ominous. You now need a licence to buy wood, so I don't suppose we'll get much benefit from our open fireplace this winter. *Please* let there be no more dreadful winters like the three in a row we've just had.

18 AUGUST

We heard on the news tonight that a foreign submarine has sunk another Swedish steamship in Swedish waters off Västervik. This is the third, or maybe even the fourth, Swedish ship to go down in similar circumstances. I'll be damned! Our letter-writers seem convinced the Germans are behind it, using Russian submarines to stir us up against Russia.

The Swedish navy is escorting the convoys and there are claims in our letters that they've sunk several subs with depth charges. We can only hope it's true. The Russians stubbornly deny any part in the deed.

A couple of spies were taken to Stockholm today, for possession of a secret radio transmitter. Father and son, the father Russian by birth. Now a Swedish citizen.

Black marketeers are getting caught every day. There's a whole other economy flourishing alongside rationing.

Churchill, whom Kar de Mumma calls 'Kurrill', has been to visit Stalin. He made the V sign while he was there, which the Russians interpreted as a promise of a second front.

The British have been having a lot of trouble in India. The Hindus are trying everything in their power to exploit the war to set themselves free (and would then give double the help to Britain, they claim) but Britain doesn't want that and Gandhi, his wife and various others have been arrested. Serious acts of violence and unrest are the order of the day.

5 SEPTEMBER
Three years of war

The war is three years old and I have not celebrated its birthday. We've all found our attitude to the war gradually changing. We used to talk about it all the time; now we see it as a necessary evil, to be thought of and talked about as little as possible. What we really *do* talk about is how little meat we get on the ration and how many eggs we've managed to lay hands on beyond our allocation, whether it'll be a cold winter, how many French beans we've managed to bottle, and so on in the same vein. Food means everything – and yet we're still well off for it. You hardly ever see meat and there's not much fish to be had, at least not in Stockholm. So when we had *roast lamb* for dinner today, it put us in quite a ceremonial mood – and it was delicious, too. I thought about the Russian and French prisoners of war in the German ports: according to letters from Swedish sailors they're on the verge of starvation and go round hunting for potato peelings in dustbins. So, whatever I may say – we don't forget the war. There's a current of despair running beneath everything all the time, and it's constantly fed by the accounts in the newspapers. In Greece there are still several thousand people dying of hunger every day; no one has the energy to bury them so they're simply thrown into a cemetery. And there's another wartime winter on the way – dear God have mercy on us. There's currently a furious battle in progress for Stalingrad; the Germans are making gains in Russia – but I'm sure nothing conclusive is going to happen before the winter. The summer is warmer than ever and in full and lovely bloom; it was pretty cold earlier on but now it's gorgeous and all the crops are ripening like mad. It's definitely going to be a good harvest this year, thank goodness.

5 OCTOBER

No no, the Germans mustn't starve! And if the Norwegian workers, who haven't set eyes on potatoes and vegetables for I don't know how long, refuse in their desperation to load the Germans' railway trucks full of food, then they get sent to concentration camps. And it's the same in all the occupied countries, of course.

But things are still going sluggishly at Stalingrad. There's not a bit of the town left in one piece, yet still the Russians aren't giving way.

A state of emergency has been declared in Trøndelag in Norway and one result is that ten Norwegian citizens were executed by firing squad at 6 p.m. on 6 October 1942 'as atonement for several sabotage attempts'. All their estates have been confiscated.

An eye for an eye, a tooth for a tooth doesn't apply any more; now wholly innocent people have to atone for crimes committed by others! Ugh, what sort of 'legal system' is that? A horrible letter in the official report describes a Norwegian who had all 32 of his healthy teeth pulled out and was then put in a concentration camp on a diet of hard bread and salt water for three months.

Just after I wrote that last entry, large numbers of Norwegians were shot.

There's nothing else particularly new to report. Stalingrad still hasn't fallen, in the desert the British have given Rommel a jolly good bashing, and the Russians are still braying for a second front, but we've seen no sign of it.

We're heading for our fourth winter of the war, and if the thought of it wearies us in Sweden, how on earth must it be for other nations? Looking back over the war, we can detect different phases in people's way of reacting: after the dreadful despair one felt at the very beginning there was a long spell of relative indifference, only interrupted by violent shocks like the occupation of Norway, the defeat of France etc. And now the real war-weariness is setting in: people are so tired of the war that they simply don't know what to do, it's all so depressing. Winter is certainly going to be pretty trying for us, at least in the cities, but one scarcely dares think how it will be in other countries. In Norway they'll be starving, for sure (the Germans take everything) and in Finland it's not much better. They say there's terrific war-weariness in Germany, particularly Berlin. In Denmark there's a rising sense of frustration; King Christian fell off his horse and nearly died but seems to be recovering now, thank goodness.

The Lindgren family celebrated Sture's 44th birthday today with a very tasty hash plus smoked eel, with cake to follow, so there's no starvation here. Not yet, at any rate.

8 NOVEMBER

In Africa, it's all gone to pot for Germany. Rommel's in disorderly retreat with the British in hot pursuit. In fact, this is the first time we've heard of real military defeat for the Germans, and many people see signs in this of an ultimate German debacle. The Italians have requested a ceasefire so they can bury their dead. What's more, the Americans have landed on the African coast, on French territory, with the result that France declared war on America today. So a few things have started happening again.

12 NOVEMBER

Things are happening! [in English]. Yesterday the Germans marched into the free zone in France, so now France is an entirely occupied country, and Pétain protested. Today he is reported to have fled. The fate of the French navy will be decided today, but according to the evening papers it intends to defend itself against any attack, so Hitler has promised not to occupy Toulon. Resistance to the Americans in Algiers has been abandoned and was probably pretty lame anyway. It must be more or less the first time the Allies have undertaken anything that has made Hitler do something he hadn't counted on. It must take a huge amount of manpower to keep France occupied, which means fewer Germans in Russia, of course. In North Africa the British march is going very fast. All these events are much better explained in the press cuttings that follow.

[Press cutting of Churchill's speech: 'European front 1942, a stratagem'. Bells to be rung to celebrate victory in Egypt.]

So different from a Hitler speech! You'd think everyone would realize that only a man with some kind of mental defect could stand up and make speeches like Hitler.

30 NOVEMBER

On Friday morning, 27 November, the entire Toulon fleet was scuttled by its own crews when the Germans tried to take France's Mediterranean base by huge military force. The crews went down with their ships. This seems to me one of the most dramatic events of the entire war. In fact, the war in general has got more and more dramatic in recent days.

So, that was that. Poor Marshal Pétain. He didn't flee after the occupation, as was claimed, but he handed all power over to that filthy little cur Laval, who obediently follows Hitler. Pétain drew up a proclamation in which he disbanded French military forces on land, on sea and in the air.

And this setback for the Germans in France comes alongside defeat to the Russians at Stalingrad; what completely lunatic amounts of blood have flowed there. I don't know how much the Russian offensive means, but the very fact that they've been able to break through the German front at various points says a great deal. One would like to feel sorry for the German soldiers, facing a Russian winter – and I do – but what *appalling* people they are. Things are shocking in Norway. Just the other day 1,000 Norwegian Jews, women and children among them, were deported to Poland and certain death. It's the work of the devil! Moreover, lots of young women have been forcibly recruited to be sent to the German soldiers up north, where they will 'primarily' be preparing meals for the soldiers, but that's doubtless just for starters! Only the other day I saw one of Hitler's dear little decrees, to the effect that the valuable Norwegian part of the Germanic racial group was to be safeguarded by taking into care any babies born to Norwegian women and fathered by German soldiers. But a poor Polish labourer who fell in love with a German girl, and had a baby with her, had to dig his own grave and was then shot in the presence of his Polish comrades, who were forced to watch as a warning.

25 DECEMBER

For us, the fourth Christmas of the war was spent in Stockholm. It was the first Christmas of my life away from Näs. But we've had such a nice time that I think we'll stay at home in future. Admittedly Karin went down with a nasty throat infection about a week before Christmas, and on the 23rd the doctor predicted it would develop into an abscess behind the tonsils, but lo and behold the crisis passed on Christmas Eve and by the evening her temperature was down and she was able to appreciate the delights of Christmas. 'Come and sit with me, Mummy, and help me enjoy being so lucky,' she said. Lars was very happy and content, too.

His presents were: ski trousers, a jacket, sports socks, ordinary socks, books, money, sweets, a photo album; and for Karin: an umbrella, a coat for school, mittens, loads of books, including *Alice in Wonderland* which she's been longing for, sweets, a couple of games, and so on. We still had tree candles this Christmas, though only Karin was allowed ten. Luckily I'd saved up a few. And there's no shortage of food. We saved our pork and bacon coupons – and this was what we were able to muster: a Christmas ham, 3½ kg, brawn, liver pâté – home-made, salt beef, veal kidney from Småland (though we got through that before Christmas). We were supposed to have a hare from Skåne as well, but it didn't come, luckily, or it would have been sheer gluttony. But we made little cakes and biscuits: ginger snaps and brandy rings, and Mother [Astrid's mother-in-law] brought lots of other kinds.

This morning we've got the Fries family coming, and they'll bring something too, so we'll have assorted meats (ham, tongue and salt beef) plus creamed potatoes, herring salad, a buckling gratin, herring, liver pâté and smoked eel. We're going to have a really nice time.

Out in the world there's nothing but misery. Things are going badly for the Germans in Russia and Africa. Major military setbacks – it must be the beginning of the end.

Pelle Dieden dropped in before Christmas and gave us news from Norway.

[Count] Pontus de la Gardie's daughter married into a Norwegian family. She told Pelle that her maternal grandfather, Count Lövenskiöld, was taken to Northern Norway as forced labour along with various other leading men of his district, in reprisal after some Norwegians in a nearby village grumbled when a German soldier pushed ahead of everybody in the cinema queue and behaved generally obnoxiously. The poor count wasn't even aware of the film performance. Such is German justice. And after the count was taken away, two trucks drove up to his grand house and a bunch of German soldiers tramped in and grabbed all they could find, including 2,000 bottles of wine, all the food that had been bottled and preserved, all the soap – they weren't even allowed to keep a scrap of soap for a baby. Then the soldiers drank themselves senseless and forced the old countess to make them tea at 3 in the morning. At Grini [the detention camp run by the Nazis in Norway], Pelle claimed to have heard from some Norwegians who had been there that they're beaten, three times a day if they're lucky, sometimes four. Woe betide them when the day of retribution comes.

And our dear parents gave us 1,000 kronor for Christmas.

1943

Christmas Eve 1943: Karin, Karolina Lindgren, Astrid and Sture.

We're just into 1943. I remember when we were children back home in Näs, we stayed up to see in 1918 and wrote 'Long live 1918' on the white wall behind the stove in our room. I wonder whether 1918 and 1943 will turn out to have anything in common; surely the war will have to end this year? I think it feels exactly like 1918. In the last few days I've heard from many directions that Sweden's situation is serious again. But I hope it's just exaggeration. And I hope there'll be peace in the world next New Year – as I've hoped every New Year these past three years.

On Christmas Eve, Admiral Darlan was murdered in Algiers.

The outlook is black for Germany. Things are going badly both in Russia and in Africa; it could be disastrous. In Germany, people are saying: *Den Krieg haben wir schon verloren* [We've already lost the war]. And I think they're right.

24 JANUARY

The situation is much as before, though things are going even worse for the Germans than they were. The British have marched into Tripoli and in Russia it looks like a sheer catastrophe. A German army is encircled at Stalingrad, over which they've fought tooth and nail. In Germany they're playing funeral music on the radio to honour the heroes of Stalingrad. Every day there are reports of the Russians advancing afresh; in the Caucasus the Germans are making a planned retreat. The poor soldiers at Stalingrad are holed up in dugouts with entrances guarded by Russian marksmen. And it's cold in Russia now. Poor people, I can't help feeling sorry for the German soldiers for having to suffer so terribly, no matter how much I detest Nazism and all the acts of violence the Germans have committed in the countries they occupied. I think the Gestapo should be expunged from the face of the earth, but there are bound to be some decent Germans too, there simply must be.

However – Sweden is tightening its defences, the king made an extremely serious throne speech at the opening of parliament and Per Albin [Hansson] made a speech that pretty much amounted to 'Don't think you can come here, or we'll soon show you otherwise!' There's a lot of talk about whether we'll get that elusive second front here this spring as part of an Allied attempt to invade Norway. If that happens one can imagine the Germans demanding transit for their troops – and us refusing (which we all hope we would do) and then all hell would be let loose. We do transport ammunition and soldiers going on leave on our Swedish railways – and even that is too much, in my view.

Sture was out with a few journalist chums the other night and Beckman at [the news agency] TT, who ought to know what he's talking about, claims Hitler's fallen into a state of total apathy. Long may it continue! If only he'd been a bit more apathetic from the start.

In Stockholm they're currently showing *Mrs Miniver*, which really is a delightful film and excellent propaganda for the Allies. It would do the Germans good to see it.

The winter thus far has been mild and still. Karin and I went skiing at Koa today.

29 JANUARY

[*Press cutting from* Dagens Nyheter *about a Swedish newspaper that spread misinformation about transit arrangements. In fact, modest numbers of German medical officers and materials were transported through Sweden in 1940, none while fighting was in progress in Norway.*]

This is really interesting, I think. Sadly there seems to be a widespread perception in Norway that we Swedes let German troops through while the fighting in Norway was still going on. It's shameful of *Göteborgs Handels- och Sjöfartstidning* to spread an assertion like that. We were scared stiff of the Germans then – April 1940 – and were standing to attention at the borders – how could we have let troops through? I don't believe it. But we did let trains through with troops on leave after the fighting stopped, and still are doing; I wish we'd stop.

Roosevelt and Churchill met in Casablanca to confer about new theatres of war. Wonder what they said about the Nordic countries?

Today the Nazis marked the tenth anniversary of their coming to power – without a speech from Hitler. According to the evening papers, Hitler was in Stalingrad to urge the surrounded troops not to surrender but to fight to the last man, because Germany's fate was in their hands. 'The Sixth Army must hold its positions to delay and obstruct the enemy advance,' Hitler decreed. In other words, their Führer has ordered them to die, and I expect they're sufficiently dutiful and pig-headed to obey.

As I said, there's been no speech from Hitler today, and that seems pretty sensational – but Göring made one instead, more than an hour late, and it went like this:

A World Gone Mad

[Press cutting, source unknown,
with long extracts in Swedish from Göring's speech.]

Imagine having the gall to stand up and tell the poor, tormented German people that 'the past ten years have demonstrated the innate power of our world view and the blessings it is able to bestow'. I wonder what the German people really think and feel, faced with the 'blessings' of National Socialism. A deadly war killing the flower of youth; the hatred and loathing of virtually all other nations; want and misery; horrific assaults on defenceless people; concerted brutalization and deculturing of its citizens, especially young people; torture, both mental and physical, of the populations of occupied countries; the informer system; the demolition of family life; the destruction of religion; 'euthanasia' for the incurably ill and mentally deficient; the reduction of love to a matter of basic procreation; the news blackout shielding them from the rest of the world and – unless all the signs are deceptive – total breakdown of the German people in the not-too-distant future. It's simply impossible for many Germans not to have realized how royally duped they've been by their Führer and other leaders. And when, as I saw in a German letter, one calls *Mrs Miniver* pure propaganda, one clearly isn't seeing very straight. A film that preaches humanity above all. I was *almost* as angry with that letter as I was with a Norwegian quisling; she claimed things have never been so free in Norway as they are now and she can't see that the Germans are getting in the way in Norway, any more than she got in the way down in Berlin last year. If you can't even see the difference *in that*, you must be a quisling or a Nazi. I've never heard anyone else make such grotesque assertions.

'There's a buzz of German and a buzz of Norwegian in the streets,' she wrote, and the dear little love thought it was so nice – and then she

130

signed off with a 'Heil Hitler – Quisling'. So the German leader took precedence over the Norwegian.

Quisling seems to have gone down with flu, so he can't receive the 'people's tribute' on his first anniversary.

Yes – and Leningrad's finally been relieved after a siege of a year and a half. You'd have to be Russian to endure the sort of suffering the population of Leningrad has had to go through. The dogs, cats and rats were all eaten up long ago, and according to Mrs Medin yesterday, she'd heard from Finland that human flesh was offered for sale towards the end – but it surely can't be true. People only had the energy to be up for a short time each day, and a lump of bread and a drop of the wateriest soup was apparently their daily ration.

From time to time we get appalling reports of Russian rampages in the Baltic during the year they were in control there. Eighty thousand people were sent to Siberia and God knows where. Had a letter from Riga today, smuggled here. The writer said we presumably wouldn't believe the accounts from there – but he swore they were true. Even women and children were shoved into cattle trucks and carried off; children were separated from their mothers, husbands and wives from each other, and so on. Rosén came the other day and said he was feeling sick; he'd seen photographs from the Baltic, and Bågstam had confirmed that she recognized several of the victims – these were pictures of actual scenes of slaughter committed by the Russians before they withdrew. No, let us *never* have to suffer the Russians here!

I must paste in Goebbels' speech and Hitler's proclamation too. Hitler's presumably having another carpet-chewing session, as he didn't speak in person.

[*Press cutting from* Dagens Nyheter: *Goebbels:*
'*The high point of our struggle is near*'.]

And here's what Hitler's proclamation said:

> [Dagens Nyheter *article from 29 January 1943:*
> *'Unambiguous victory' promised by the Führer.*]

There would be plenty to say about the above, but I think Johannes Wickman's comments in *Dagens Nyheter* will do the job:

> [*Press cutting from* Dagens Nyheter *from 31 January*
> *1943 of Wickman's piece 'Jubilee without jubilation'.*]

Say what you will about Wickman – but he's not exactly neutral. I wonder what would happen if the Gestapo got hold of him.

The only thing I don't like is the general tendency of Anglophiles to make the Russians into little doves of peace. I think we are going to discover that they are *not*.

7 MARCH

No major news to report. But one remarkable thing is the total reorganization of the German economy, making *everything* subordinate to the aims of the war. The occupied countries are starting to do the same, too. The other day there was a huge British air raid over Berlin, in which Zarah Leander's villa was totally destroyed. Many hundreds killed.

Save the Children has launched a big drive to help the children of Europe – and they certainly need it. But Karin had put on a kilo at her last check-up and now weighs 29kg.

In Denmark there was an abortive bomb attack on German women. I can't recall if I ever wrote about King Christian's Hitler telegram.

They say the clampdown in Germany's treatment of Denmark is the direct result of this telegram. Anyway: Hitler sent the Danish king a telegram – I forget exactly when – it must have been for his birthday. The telegram was in the usual bombastic style, all about the new European order, etc. The telegram Christian sent in reply, with heart-breaking Danishness, read as follows: 'Mange Tak Christian Rex' [Many thanks Christian Rex]. No wonder Hitler was furious. Our newspapers only dropped hints about 'the brief royal telegram', giving no details. I heard the rest from Gunnar at Christmas.

And then there were presidential elections in Finland. Ryti was re-elected. He had a lot of trouble forming his government.

Yesterday there was a terrible accident at [the military training ground at] Ränneslätt. A charge of TNT exploded, seven soldiers were killed, six of them outright and another died later, and many were badly hurt. There are a lot of accidents even in our peaceable defence forces.

Hitler is staying silent and speaking only through deputies. Some say he's dead, others that he's lost his mind.

I APRIL

In Africa, the British have stormed the Mareth Line and it's not looking good for Rommel. We haven't heard much from Russia: things are probably going badly for all of them. Hitler's come back to life again after his long silence and made a speech or two. But German disintegration is in all probability only a question of time.

Here in Sweden there's been a lot of hot air and questioning in parliament about a German courier plane that had to come down in the water at Lekvattnet, which produced a worrying lack of reaction from the Swedish armed forces, except for a 17-year-old member of the home guard, who has received a medal for his resourcefulness. The 'courier plane' was full of German soldiers and had machine guns on board, albeit not assembled. The affair has caused a lot of displeasure in Britain.

Allied invasion is anticipated in one place and another, before too long. In Denmark, acts of sabotage have increased dramatically.

The British bombing raids on Germany and Italy are having an impact.

GOOD FRIDAY

A week ago, most probably on Friday the 16th, the Swedish submarine *Ulven* disappeared with its 33-man crew. The sub had been taking part in naval exercises down on the west coast and was last seen on Thursday afternoon. The *Ulven* didn't appear on Friday for its scheduled exercises and investigations began. A week has passed since then, in which the interest of the whole Swedish nation has been focused exclusively on the *Ulven*. All hope is now lost. It's assumed that the sub got into such trouble that it was stranded on the seabed, unable to manoeuvre, its crew still alive for as long as their oxygen lasted. All possible resources were put into *looking* for it, with all the expertise that Swedish science can [illegible word], and in the end the anguished father of one of the crew paid for a flight to bring down Karlsson, the clairvoyant from Ankarsund in Västerbotten. But not even the clairvoyant could locate the *Ulven*. The weather's been dreadful, one storm after another, which stopped the divers going down. Things looked really hopeful to begin with. The papers declared that the *Ulven* had been 'localized', but by God that didn't mean they'd found it. There were reports of knock-ings heard from the *Ulven*, but as none of them were in Morse code, I don't think they really came from the submarine. Today's paper says: 'At 6 on Tuesday morning the last knocking was heard on the hydrophones – since then there has been silence.' As this would more or less correspond to the length of time the crew could be assumed to have stayed alive, it does make you wonder.

On Sunday evening the Swedish submarine *Draken* reported that on the Friday morning, that is, the day the *Ulven* vanished, and in the same waters, it was fired on by an armed German merchant vessel. The commander of the *Draken*, the prize blockhead, didn't tell anyone until Sunday evening. Protests have been lodged in Berlin with a demand for a prompt investigation of whether the same merchant vessel shot at the *Ulven*. We can only hope that this was the case and that the men aboard *Ulven* died a quick death rather than enduring a week's horrendous suffering. But if it turns out that the German ship, which is called the *Altkirch* by the way, sank the sub in a way that left parts of it watertight and the crew still alive, then I hope they kill the commander of the *Draken* who couldn't spit out what he knew until the Sunday evening.

The navy has suffered a great tragedy, much worse than Hårsfjärden in my view. I read a moving letter from a sailor; he wrote that he and his fellow seamen were sitting round talking about the *Ulven* 'and there wasn't a single one of us not in tears'.

Today spring seems to have arrived in earnest! And the *Ulven* men will never get to see another spring. The commanding officer had been married just over a year and his wife is expecting their first child any day now.

In England, Churchill has announced that intelligence has reached them about German intentions to use gas on the eastern front. Churchill is preparing the Germans for the fact that if this is true, gas will immediately be released over German port cities and war-related industrial sites. This is going to be a lovely spring and no mistake.

But today out at Djurgården among wood anemones and yellow star of Bethlehem in the sunshine it was glorious. Lars has gone to Småland, so it was just Sture, Karin and me. Karin and I played 'golden shoes and golden hat', which you had to undergo various trials to win. On the subject of golden shoes: today we'll hear about shoe rationing, and if the papers are to be believed it's going to be more than somewhat strict. I'm so annoyed I didn't at least get Karin's shoes half-soled for Easter.

9 MAY

Since I last wrote, here's more or less what has happened. We've had a reply to our protest about the *Draken* and it's a damned cheeky one, see below:

[Unidentified press cutting.]

Just the sort of insolence you'd expect from those bastards. So Germany's to have the right to decide how our Swedish subs behave in *Swedish* waters! But we responded in no uncertain terms, probably in sharper tones than we've ever dared before. The Germans said nothing about the *Ulven* in their memo.

This was the Swedish government response:

[Unidentified press cutting.]

I suppose the most disquieting thing of all was that the damned Germans laid a minefield in Swedish waters. It was probably that minefield which decided the *Ulven*'s fate. Because the other day *they found the Ulven*, for which they'd hunted so intently and desperately. And it was lying more or less in the middle of that mine belt at a depth of 52 metres. They still haven't found out how it met its end, but it doesn't seem to have had a collision or been fired on. The bow looked 'compressed', said the divers who went down. It was a fishing boat that found it. All are eager to find out whether the crew died instantaneously, which seems likeliest and what we all wish and hope for. Presumably it hit a German mine, and in *Swedish* waters. So now it must be time to stop the hateful transit permits to Germans 'going on leave', which the whole Swedish nation is furious about.

Another development: the 'safe conduct by sea', which the Germans stopped in January, was reinstated a few days ago. Perhaps we can start getting some essentials in again, a bit of coffee and some shoe leather so they can relax the strict shoe rationing slightly.

Well everything I've written here has been about Sweden. But of course there's been plenty going on in the wider war as well. Tunis and Bizerte have fallen, so the game is up for the Axis in North Africa. This is a success of the first order for the Allies, of course, their greatest of the war so far. The remains of the Axis army are squeezed into a tight corner on the Cap Bon peninsula and thousands upon thousands have surrendered.

There's also been quite a row, which I haven't really followed, between the Russian and Polish governments. I didn't even know there *was* a Polish government, but I presume it's based in London. Anyway, the Polish government has demanded an investigation, through the Red Cross, of some dreadful mass graves in Katyn (I think it was called), where the Russians killed and buried 10,000 Polish officers after they annexed Poland. Yes, God preserve us from the Russians! They've also been rowing about Poland's future borders and relations with Russia, but as I say, I haven't been paying attention.

So warm and so lovely, what a blessing! Unbelievably good weather. The day before yesterday, Karin turned nine. Elsa-Lena and Matte were here. Karin got a watch, a school bag, a box of chocolates, one book, one pair of overtrousers from us, and several books from our visitors. For dinner we had not only Matte but also prawns, radishes, sardines, ham and eggs, and the rest of the cake.

Lars took his English exam the same day, which will decide his final mark in the subject. A school year is drawing to an end, thank goodness, because it's all been quite a trial since he had those warnings from school [about potentially poor grades], and I'm sure I've nagged more than I should. He's bound to fail his German; as for the other subjects, we can only hope and pray for the best.

I'm back at work on Monday after a delightful week and a half off for a terrible cold. While I was in bed I wrote a few odds and ends and sent them in, first to *Stockholms-Tidningen*, which bought one of my light articles and returned three, then to *Dagens Nyheter*, which returned both the pieces I'd sent them. On one of them, Staffan Tjerneld had written some comments, starting with 'The girl can write, there's no question about it,' but it was too short and not true enough to life, hah hah!

Enough of this drivel. A minor detail such as Stalin dissolving the Comintern probably deserves a mention. It was in the papers yesterday and has caused a great stir all round the world, of course. It would mean that Bolshevism has renounced the idea of world revolution. I very much doubt that's the case; the Comintern will still exist but under cover, and the whole device has probably just been dreamt up to curry favour with public opinion in Britain and America.

I can't remember if I wrote that the British bombed two so-called barrages in Germany, resulting in huge destruction and large-scale flooding.

A German Jew in exile is said to have given the British the idea, which will now be the excuse for fresh persecution of the Jews in Germany.

That's all for today.

3 JUNE

No particular news from the war, I don't think. Something called 'Attu', which the Japanese held, has fallen. When the few hundred warriors who were left realized they wouldn't make it, they turned to face the Imperial Palace in Tokyo, bowed deeply and then charged the enemy with one last banzai cry, to be mown down to the last man, according to the papers. So much for 'Attu' – I don't know what the implications are in the general chaos.

The bombing is more devastating than ever. At work I saw an Italian propaganda photo – a maternity hospital in Italy had been bombed and the picture showed many dead and maimed – it was simply awful.

In the papers the other day they said that, in all, 100,000 people in Athens are dying of hunger. Sixteen hundred a day, when things are at their worst.

But in Sweden we're doing remarkably well on the food front, a very distinct improvement. Lots of meat and bacon and there's suddenly fish available, so they've lifted fish rationing. It's really easy to be a housewife now. Butter's the only tricky thing.

Ascension Day was fine and the warmer weather arrived and I was angry as heck with Sture for the *usual reason* [in English], so I went out cycling with Karin, in the morning with Alli and in the afternoon (after dinner) just the two of us, to Koa. It's so beautiful now, the lilacs and chestnuts are blooming like mad. I wanted Lasse to come with us too, but he prefers to go his own way nowadays.

Such a gorgeous Whitsun Eve, and so hot. Everything's abnormally early this year. Here we are in our living room with the windows wide open, and it's more or less like sitting in the park. The sounds are intensely summery: the clack of heels on the pavement outside, the noise of the children in the park, and when the trams speed by it sounds almost as if they are coming straight in here.

Karin's gone out to Solö [in the Stockholm archipelago] with Matte and I'm glad she's there for this heatwave, even though it feels rather empty at home without her. She had her exam on the 8th and got Ba [a satisfactory pass] in all her subjects except music and gymnastics. Lars, on the other hand, came home with a sorry set of results (Bc [a bare pass] maths, B? [a pass?] in English, history, chemistry and French), which is such a shame after he got such good marks last year. He doesn't seem to have realized he's in upper secondary school now. He had some work as a bicycle messenger this week and earned 50 kronor, and next week he and Göran are off on a cycle trip. I wish I could go with them because the summer's so glorious it makes you want to get out of town instantly. But – it can't be denied that it's extremely lovely here, in the most beautiful summer city on this earth (so I think, though I haven't seen that many others) and all I want to do is get out on my bike in the evenings to enjoy the profusion of flowers and all the greenery, the floral scents and the totally fantastic evening sky. The season of rapture, and I certainly am enraptured!

We marked the start of Whitsun with a dinner of radishes, hard-boiled eggs with anchovies, asparagus, veal chops and mazarin tarts. It's beyond belief that we're suddenly so well off for food; it's the simplest thing in the world to be a housewife, though expensive, of course.

Meanwhile, the Italian island of Pantelleria has capitulated after a devastating bombardment. 'You keep writing and writing,' says Sture.

'Are you writing about Lampedusa?' Lampedusa is the next island the Allies will take. The mood in Italy must be lower than low. After all, the occupation of Pantelleria can be seen as a little prelude to invasion, since it was originally Italian territory. There's a lot of talk of invasion these days.

Today the papers say the report on the 1941 Hårsfjärden accident indicates that the cause of the disaster appears to be sabotage. How horrible!

In Russia, the Germans and Russians are preparing to go on the offensive. In Germany, the Allies are continuing their dreadful bombing, last night targeting Düsseldorf and Münster, Wilhelmshaven and Cuxhaven in what's said to be the biggest bombing raid yet. I read in a letter from a pilot today that in Germany they claim 200,000 people died when the barrages were blown up a while back. The British pilots who carried out the bombing were apparently specially trained for a month for the mission. The devastation being visited on the world is just growing and growing. The sanctity of life is held in contempt. In this delightful summertime [first line of a Swedish hymn]…

2 JULY

Since I last wrote, the king has managed to turn 85, a landmark that's attracted a lot of press coverage here and abroad. There was great excitement in Stockholm on the day and it was all very festive, but I was so busy getting Lasse's kit ready for the cycle trip that I didn't even get a chance to go and see the procession through town. It was as dry as tinder all through the early summer and we were desperate for rain, but why did it have to rain *partout* at precisely 5 p.m. on 16 June when the king was in his open carriage? Yet it did, of course, and everybody worried because the king was getting wet. He's incredibly popular, our old king, and the whole world sent him congratulatory telegrams. The

Swedish people are convinced it's King Gustaf we have to thank for our country not being at war, and it's entirely possible that they are right.

Then it was midsummer. Lars and Göran's cycle trip took them round Östergötland and Småland. Karin was out at Solö and had her ride in the hay cart as promised, but came home with Sigge Gullander on the evening of Midsummer Day. Sture and I took a bike ride out to Saltsjöbaden and had a really nice time.

That was followed by a couple of hectic days while I got everything ready for Karin and me to go off to Småland, which we did on the 27th. And now we're here, and the children are enjoying it to the full, as am I.

The war continues more or less as usual. An American offensive in the Pacific, they said on the radio news this morning. Invasion, invasion, invasion, they can't stop talking about it, and what they mean is an Allied invasion on the continent – not like 1940, when 'invasion' meant a German invasion of Britain, which we were expecting any minute, but it never came. *That* was when Hitler should have mounted his invasion, when he had his big chance, but he missed it.

Anyway, we haven't seen any invasion yet, though things look rather ominous in Sicily. The Allied bombing continues, with feeble resistance from the Axis. Cologne Cathedral, probably Germany's finest piece of architecture, has suffered bomb damage and the German newspapers are yelling about British vandalism – but what did they do in 1940?

17 JULY

There have been major developments since last time, but our busy days in Småland left me no time to write about them. It started with a big Russian offensive, with massive bloodshed on both sides. At Kursk, I think it was called. Then a few days after that big battle started, the

Allies pulled off a landing on Sicily, where there's now heavy fighting. It said on the news that the Allies are only 10km from Catania and it's surely only a matter of time until all resistance is beaten down. After that it'll probably be the mainland's turn, I expect. I suppose you could call this the start of the much-vaunted invasion. The Allies are dropping leaflets over Italy, urging the Italian people to sue for peace.

I forgot to write about our phenomenon Gunder Hägg, who's in America and running like the blazes. He's run three races, all at different distances – and though he didn't beat his own world records he beat his American opponents. 'Gunder the Wonder,' they call him – and tonight he's running his fourth race. We all take a keen interest in his success and he's considered a first-rate ambassador for Sweden in the USA at the moment.

Sture, Karin and I arrived here in Furusund the day before yesterday. Lars is still in Småland, busy with farming, German and maths. We picked our first chanterelles yesterday. Summer isn't very reliable this year, you have to seize the moment. And now I'm off to bed to read a bit of All världens berättare [Storytellers Around the World]; today it's [Maupassant's] 'Ball of Fat'.

25 JULY

Well, as the following newspaper cuttings show, Hitler and Musso had a meeting, and Rome got bombed. The assumption is that Hitler wanted to see Musso to stop him making a separate peace deal. 'Italy chooses the path of honour', the Italian papers said as a riposte to the leaflets – but there are peace rallies going on in the country and the people want peace. On Sicily the Allies are moving forward little by little; it's going terribly well, Churchill says. In an order of the day issued on Saturday,

Stalin declared that Germany's July offensive had been stopped and 70,000 Germans had fallen. Berlin doesn't consider the summer offensive to have reached its peak yet. The number of Russians killed is put at a third of a million. Even if both sides are telling packs of lies, you can't help being petrified at the thought of all the human misery behind it.

Recently I've been reading in Grimberg's history of the world about ancient Rome and all the bloodbaths and atrocities, proscriptions and wars of conquest. Reading the papers and coming across the same geographical names, one simply despairs at how little humanity has learnt in the intervening centuries.

In spite of everything people have started to hope, not tomorrow, perhaps not this year, but at least not in some hopelessly distant future. And Italy's going to collapse pretty soon, everyone thinks so.

And then Gunder Hägg ran his best US race yet – an English mile in 4.05.3.

And summer's really arrived now. Sture, Karin and I have been making the most of it here in Furusund: we row to our bathing island in the mornings and Linnéa and I pick berries in the afternoons. Lasse's still in Småland and I miss him like mad, especially in the evenings. But he's happiest there, and he's coming over for a brief stay in a week's time, before he and I go back to town to get down to the German and maths. Karin swims like a little fish now and is thrilled that she's bold enough to throw herself in pretty much anywhere.

[*Press cuttings. One undated and unidentified: 'The Allied message to the people of Italy'. Roosevelt and Churchill appeal to them to surrender.* Dagens Nyheter, *21 July 1943: 'Axis leaders reject enemy speculation'. Envoy Dr Schmidt threatens 'vengeful retaliation' –* Astrid heads this cutting 'Crap'. Dagens Nyheter, *the same day: After the bombing of Rome, petrol is free and loaded vehicles stream out of the city.*]

I wrote that last night. But on the radio this morning we heard the really sensational news: *Mussolini has been dismissed* by [King] Victor Emmanuel and Marshal Badoglio has been appointed his successor. Hey ho! Tiddley pom and fiddle-de-dee! The hydra of Fascism has lost its head. Now – now – *now* perhaps humanity is starting on the road to recovery of its full health. That bastard who (having shaken some life into those Italians, one has to admit) despatched the peaceable Italian people to Abyssinia on a war of conquest in 1935, initiating all these years of unrest, who once there unleashed gas attacks on defenceless natives, who thanks to his intervention in Spain prolonged the terrible civil war and who, incidentally, by creating Fascism, also provided the conditions for that civil war, and also the conditions, or to be more precise, the model, for National Socialism in Germany, which in turn caused this most terrible world war of all time – this grand bastard has now been sent off into a corner to await the verdict of history, which will assuredly be harsh. Phew! That was a long sentence, but we're talking about world history here. They say he's ill, stomach cancer, and if anybody deserves stomach cancer, it has to be him.

So that was Benito Mussolini! Could it be Hitler next please?

Prime Minister Churchill's statement in the House of Commons on Tuesday, on the situation in Italy, began like this:

'The House will have heard with satisfaction of the downfall of one of the principal criminals of this desolating war. The end of Mussolini's long and severe reign over the Italian people undoubtedly marks the close of an epoch in the life of Italy. The keystone of the Fascist arch has crumbled, and without attempting to prophesy, it does not seem unlikely that the entire Fascist edifice will fall to the ground in ruins, if it has not already so fallen.'

29 JULY

The Fascist Party has been dissolved. Serious unrest in Milan. Running battles in the streets. Many civilians and soldiers killed. The masses are demanding immediate peace. The military arsenal stormed. Demonstrations in support of the Soviet Union.

An American newspaper correspondent called Victor Emmanuel 'a moronic little king', which upset Roosevelt.

4 AUGUST

Today there was a memorial service for the crew of the *Ulven*, which has finally been brought up from the watery grave where it has been lying since April. Five died of mine injuries (German mine in Swedish waters, of course) and the rest drowned – a quick death, that is – and thank God for that.

And Sibylla had her fourth princess last night.

6 AUGUST

Finally, finally they're stopping the transit arrangements that the whole Swedish nation has detested so much. I expect *Göteborgs Handels- och Sjöfartstidning* and *Trots Allt* will be shouting for joy, they fought like lions! After all, this breach of neutrality was forced on us and it gives us a clear sense of Germany's current weakness that it's granted us 'permission' to stop the wretched business. In Norway there's been huge bitterness against us because of the transits and the view there is most definitely that they started while the war in Norway was still going on. I hope and believe that our government's firm denial of this is a true reflection of what happened.

God knows whether the war is actually going to end soon, all the same! Germany's debacle is hanging in the air, so to speak. Things are going lousily in Russia, the Russians have taken Orel, in Sicily Catania has fallen and it's soon going to be a Tunis in miniature. Italy hasn't given up, however, even though the people are demonstrating and demanding peace. The dreadful bombing of Germany goes on; one can't help weeping over the accounts from Hamburg, just think, there are still children there, it's heart-rending, terrible, unbearable. I've just read Jean-Jacques Agapit's book [*Dites-le 'leur'* (*Tell 'Them'*)], an account of the hell that wounded French prisoners of war went through at a German hospital. The whole book is drowning in blood and pus and I'm now so *fed up* [in English] with everything war-related that I haven't the words for it. And how must it be in the countries where they have those atrocities right in front of their eyes on a daily basis? It's a good book, but still didn't make such an impression on me as Remarque's *All Quiet on the Western Front*, which came out between these two world wars. When I was reading it, I would creep under the covers at night (this was at Atlasgatan) and shed tears of despondency, and I remember thinking that if there was ever another war and Sweden thought of joining in, I would go on my knees to the government and *implore* them not to let all hell break loose. I would shoot Lars myself rather than let him go to war, I thought. How they must suffer, the poor mothers on this insane planet. When I thought of the crew of the *Ulven* and when I read Agapit's book, I tried to imagine my Lars on the sunken submarine (when we thought they were trapped on the seabed, still alive) or in a fever with suppurating wounds in a war hospital, and simply imagining it was so agonizing I could hardly endure it! So how must it feel to those for whom such things aren't imagination but cruel reality? How can it be possible that humanity has to suffer such torment and why do we have war? Does it really take no more than a couple of individuals like Hitler and Mussolini to drive a whole world into destruction and chaos? Please, please, *please* let it be over soon, the bloodshed at least; then there's bound to be all the other misery that follows in the wake of war. Grandmother goes around these days all perky and optimistic and thinks that as soon as we have peace, everything will be all right again. She seems sure humanity will be happy as long as the coffee starts flowing again and rationing is scrapped, here and abroad, but the utterly desperate wounds left by the war aren't going to be healed by a drop of coffee. Peace can't give mothers back their sons, or the little children of Hamburg and Warsaw back their lives. The hatred doesn't end the day peace comes, those whose relations have been tormented to death in German concentration camps won't forget anything just because there's peace and the memory of the thousands of children who starved to death in Greece will most certainly still be in their mothers' hearts, if those mothers themselves survived. All the war-wounded will still be limping about with a leg or an arm missing, those who lost their sight are still just as blind and those whose nervous systems were torn to shreds in the inhuman tank battles will not recover, either, just because peace arrives. But still, but still – please let peace come soon, so people can gradually start coming back to their senses.

And yet – what is peace going to look like? What will happen to poor Finland? And will Bolshevism, with all the terror and tyranny it implies, be given free rein in Europe? Those who have already lost their lives in this war could turn out to be the most fortunate.

Summer 1943 is drawing to a close – or perhaps it's just how I see it, since my summer leave is over. Tomorrow Lars and I go to Stockholm. The weather here in Furusund has been fine and warm, but today it rained and felt quite autumnal in every way. Karin and Linnéa are going to stay on for a while. Karin's finally overcome her fear of swimming in deep water. She's also learnt to jump from the springboard on the jetty, to her own huge gratification. Lars is coming back to re-sit his German and maths. We've had various clashes while we've been together this summer because he's so averse to studying in the holidays.

[Typed transcript of a letter from Astrid's work at the censor's office from Norway about hatred and revenge propaganda, terrible treatment inflicted by the Nazis and a call for the Norwegian people to swear a solemn oath never to forget Gestapo terror. Also a press cutting from Dagens Nyheter, *15 August 1943:* 'Huge losses on both sides in the Battle of Orel'.*]*

That's all for today!

26 AUGUST

As has been reported – Roosevelt and Churchill met in Quebec. Stalin wasn't there, the little squirt. It caused a great sensation when Litvinov, Russia's ambassador to Washington, was suddenly called home and replaced by someone else. This has been interpreted as a sign that the Russians and the other two Allied partners have fallen out with each other. Russia wants a second front, and as such they will accept nothing but an invasion across the Channel. Every amateur pundit has something to say these days about the possibility of a separate peace between Germany and Russia, which would really put Britain and America in a spot. For Germany, it would probably be the only way out of a collapse that looks imminent. The bombing of Berlin has started and is expected to proceed much as in Hamburg.

There's been a lot of unrest in Denmark of late, loads of sabotage and out-and-out clashes between Germans and Danes, especially in Odense.

After lots of intensive revision with me, Lars re-sat his German and maths and made it into the next year. Karin's started in year three and got a new 'Miss', Mrs Adin, who seems to be quite sharp and not all that young. To celebrate Lars getting through, he and I went with Karin's express permission to the 7 p.m. show at the pictures. Sture got home at 8.30 to find Karin crying bitterly. She'd started her homework, revising her times tables, and found that in her sleepy state she didn't know them. So then she sat up with Sture until I got back at 9.30, and threw herself into my arms in tears. But I soon consoled her. Then she fell asleep and forgot the whole affair. She couldn't escape a little throat infection before school started, and today I'm in bed with a tickly sore throat. But I shall get up in a little while and pop down to NK [department store] to buy some blouse fabric for Karin and some material to repair my fur with. We're also going to bottle 10kg of French beans, so the day won't be wasted.

THIS EVENING

There are reports in *Aftonbladet* of major disturbances in Denmark. I'll cut out the piece.

I forgot to save it. But today we heard that a state of emergency has been declared in Denmark. Yesterday telephone lines with Denmark were cut, and here in Sweden we were seriously worried about what was happening. Today we've had the explanation. The Danish government was given an ultimatum to restore order in the country, which has been jeopardized recently by sabotage, strikes, street riots and the like. As the government didn't consider itself able to succeed, a state of emergency was imposed. Anyone who argues is hauled up in front of a German court martial; strikes or incitement to strike are punishable by death. All gatherings of people are prohibited, as is all traffic after dark. Traffic between Sweden and Denmark has been halted (and there's us with the Danish national athletics team in Stockholm today). Communication by telephone – and telegraph – is still blocked. I bet it's going to be as hellish in Denmark as in Norway.

A Swedish civil plane, the *Gladan*, on a flight from England to Sweden under Captain Lindner vanished last Friday and hasn't been heard of since. It was probably shot down. Swedish fishing boats off the west coast, which were peacefully fishing in international waters as they always have, came under machine-gun fire from a German merchant vessel. Twelve fishermen are missing.

King Boris of Bulgaria died yesterday, officially from angina pectoris (just back from a conference with Hitler), but according to the rumours shot in the abdomen by a police inspector. He is succeeded by his six-year-old son, Simeon II.

So this has been the state of affairs in Denmark since Sunday 29 July 1943. I must definitely paste in the proclamation of the state of emergency as well!

[Press cutting from Dagens Nyheter, *30 August 1943:*
'Regulations for the state of emergency in Denmark'.]

30 AUGUST

I think they're running completely wild in Denmark. Just listen:

[Astrid's following comments are interspersed between pasted-in
press cuttings. Dagens Nyheter, *30 August 1943: 'Nine Danish*
ships flee to Sweden, the rest sunk'. 'Copenhagen naval port blown
up'. 'Battle for the Lifeguards' barracks'. "I'm a dead man,"
declared Denmark's civilian Nazi administrator Dr Best after visit
to Berlin. 'Danish government under German military guard'.]

Mussolini's daughter and son-in-law seem to have got away.

[Unidentified cutting.]

Eleven Norwegians have been executed for spying.

Germany has sent a ludicrously caustic reply to our protest about
the shooting of Swedish fishing boats:

[Press cutting from Dagens Nyheter, *30 August 1943:*
'Sharp response from Berlin to fishermen's protest'.]

And the Germans are furious with the Swedish press for stirring up
agitation against Germany. Which it is, in fact.

[Press cutting from Dagens Nyheter, *30 August*
1943: 'PS The Swedish press is spiteful'.]

A rather silly article about Mussolini by *Dagens Nyheter*'s Rome correspondent:

[Press cutting from Dagens Nyheter, *30 August 1943: 'Dictator's bathing-resort flirtation turned into idyllic triangle drama'.]*

I SEPTEMBER

[Unidentified press cuttings about Denmark with a map (the eastern edge showing Spain, Portugal and Ireland is missing)]

I put in the truncated map above just to show how poor little Sweden is squeezed in Germany's grip, just like Switzerland. But notwithstanding that, we're cursing and swearing at Germany, we and the Swiss. The map in its original state showed how pitifully few European countries have been able to stay out of the war: Sweden, Switzerland, Spain, Portugal and Éire. Seeing the map, you really understand what an extraordinary blessing it is that we still have peace, and are so well off in every way, for now, with the war passing its fourth anniversary and our neighbours up here in the north in such dire straits.

In Denmark it really is infernal. The mass arrests go on. Postal and telephone links are still cut.

This war has now lasted almost as long as the last one, so it's *got* to end. On 11 December 1943 there ought to be an armistice, if it's to be exactly the same number of years and months as the last world war.

5 SEPTEMBER

The day before yesterday, the 3rd, exactly four years since Britain declared war on Germany, the Eighth Army crossed the Strait of

Messina and landed on the 'toe' of Italy. As I write this, things are progressing rapidly, several bridgeheads have been secured and the Italian population is coming out with white sheets as a sign of surrender. The Germans are presumably getting ready to defend a line further north. Italy, of course, wants nothing better than to get the Germans out of the country so it can capitulate in peace and quiet. The kids are kicking up a rumpus, so I can't write any more, but these certainly are thrilling times.

Well, Karin picked up *Aftonbladet* and Lars is sitting reading, so I can write that it's been a glorious day of brilliant sunshine. Karin and I cycled across Norra Djurgården to Djurgårdsbrunn and then went home and had roast chicken for dinner. Sture's sitting in the armchair at the moment, fast asleep and snoring, while the children and I read my war diaries. Then Karin's off to bed and I shall read her some of *In Search of the Castaways*, and after that I shall enjoy settling down with Churchill's *My Early Life*.

9 SEPTEMBER

Yesterday evening when I was perched on the edge of Karin's bed reading her *In Search of the Castaways*, Lars barged in and told us that Italy's agreed to unconditional surrender. It was expected, but it nonetheless felt rather special to experience a red-letter day in this war, and I gave both children a 25-öre coin as a memento. The proud Axis is dislocated and in Germany many a bitter word has been spoken of treachery, with much cursing of Victor Emmanuel in particular. And of Badoglio, too. The ceasefire was signed back on 3 September on Sicily, but has been kept secret, presumably so the Italian fleet would have time to get into Allied ports.

How long can the Germans hang on? Things are going wretchedly in Russia, really wretchedly, and now the Allies will have a firm foothold in Italy and perhaps in the Balkans as well, before long.

Numerous death sentences have been passed in Denmark. And they aren't getting any Swedish newspapers any more; it's one affliction after another. Large numbers are escaping to Sweden.

IO SEPTEMBER

It's not much fun in Italy. The Germans have occupied Rome, according to this evening's radio news, plus other parts of the country, so now the Germans and Italians are fighting each other as well as the Allies. King Victor Emmanuel is said to have abdicated in favour of his son Umberto. Crown Princess Marie José has apparently fled the country with her four children. What's more, the Germans have occupied Albania, where they were expecting an Allied invasion. Those long-suffering Italians deserve our pity, poor devils. I expect they thought things would finally calm down now, but then they got even worse.

20 SEPTEMBER

Terrible for Germany on all fronts. In Italy it came to a battle at Salerno, which initially looked as if it was going down the drain for the Allies and was proclaimed by the Germans to be the new Dunkirk, but which has now evidently been won by the Allies, though with major losses. And in Russia things are looking disastrous for the Germans.

Why can't that disgusting man keep his mouth shut? Italy is in a wretched predicament, with the Germans and the Allies fighting like mad over its territory and Italians joining in on both sides. And then Musso wants them to spill even more blood to blot out the disgrace. He could spill his own, if you ask me.

On Thursday evening just as I was going to bed, around 10 because I was tired after the day's mushrooming excursion, the phone rang – and it was Esse. He'd travelled from Copenhagen early that afternoon and he dashed over to see us straight off the train. The Swedish consul in Copenhagen strongly advised all Swedish citizens to get back home, and Esse is in fact a Swedish citizen, even though he doesn't speak any Swedish. Just imagine, it took a world war to get him home to Sweden. It was a very self-assured and go-getting young man who stepped into our flat, with extremely affected manners. He couldn't stop talking about the current situation in Denmark, and it was a tale of sabotage and misery. He claims all the young people in Denmark are 'illegal' and join in the sabotage. Esse himself told Lasse that he'd helped to blow up a factory, dressed in German uniform. It's understandable that the young people are throwing themselves fervently into patriotic activities, but it certainly isn't entirely for the good. Doubtless the destructive tendencies that are in everyone will be stirred up alarmingly, and it won't be so easy afterwards to go back to a normal life where blowing up factories and smashing windows isn't encouraged.

26 SEPTEMBER

The other day, Eden said more in the House of Commons about Hess's mission to Britain. It *was* a peace plan he brought over. This boiled down to Britain being granted a free hand in its empire in return for Germany getting free hands on the continent; the German colonies would be returned, Russia would be banished to Asia. If Britain didn't agree to peace on these terms, Germany would totally crush them and keep Britain in subjugation for evermore. Hess claimed to have set off without Hitler's consent, but it would be Hitler's intentions he put forward, at any rate.

Smolensk has fallen! Kiev is bound to be next. And the Russians will probably soon drive the Germans over the border.

3 OCTOBER

In Denmark, the Germans are now persecuting the Jews. Several thousand are to be deported. The Swedish government has lodged a strong protest in Berlin and also offered to take in all the Danish Jews. It probably won't achieve anything. In the meantime, huge numbers of Jews are fleeing over to here.

Naples is in Allied hands. It'll be Rome's turn soon.

We've got to save gas now, and the result is that we've got our hot water back. There's no describing how nice that is and how much easier it's made the housework. See below a touching observation on the hot-water question, a cutting from *Söndagsnissestrix*.

> *[Press cutting of a cartoon, 3 October 1943. One grubby little boy says to another: 'So that's the end of all our fun'.]*

10 OCTOBER

The proclamation overleaf by some dependable old Nazi is pretty symptomatic of the turn of the tide in recent days. It also says a good deal about the great indignation in Sweden at the treatment of the Jews in Denmark. Jewish refugees are currently coming across [the strait of] Øresund in droves. It actually looks as though the Germans aren't bothering to try to stop them. We've apparently got 6,000 Danish refugees, mostly Jews, in the country. The Swedish anti-Semites are having a field day, distributing leaflets that call the refugees a collection of murderers and rapists.

These past few days I've been so cast down by Rut's tragedy. Thursday was when it happened and it's so dreadful that I refuse to believe it. Yesterday they released her and she's got to wait three weeks for the verdict. I spoke to her on the phone today and I've never heard a voice so brutally broken. And it's another tragedy that can be ascribed to the war, because if there hadn't been a war, she'd never have had this job, and if she hadn't had this job, she wouldn't have been exposed to such shocking temptation.

> *[Press cuttings from Aftonbladet: vitriolic Nazi complaints about the Swedish press; new Italian minister has to swear allegiance to God and Mussolini; a long article by Karl Olivecrona about the persecution of the Jews in Denmark.]*

20 OCTOBER

I forgot to write that Italy, Badoglio's Italy, that is, declared war on Germany a few days ago. And today it says in the paper that Mussolini's going to draw back. Quite right, too. Germany's Russian front has been broken. There's an exchange of British and German prisoners of war through Swedish mediation in Göteborg.

I've included this photograph of the exchange of POWs just for the soldier's face. To me, it expresses all the yearning of every soldier around the world.

[*Photo from* Aftonbladet, *20 October 1943,
caption: 'A young Englishwoman, married to
a Swedish sailor, found her brother and was
able to talk to him for a few minutes'.*]*

24 OCTOBER

In the early hours of Friday morning an Aerotransport plane, the *Gripen*, was shot down off Smögen, by (it was later established) a German Junker. The *Gripen* continued to fly for 20 minutes after it was fired on but then a fuel tank exploded, the plane came down in flames and crashed into a cliff face. Thirteen passengers were killed, two were rescued, two Russian diplomats' wives, each with two children, were found to be among the passengers. The plane's captain and first officer both leave wives and young children. And after the board meeting last Sunday, Sture came home beaming with delight to announce that he's to fly to England for work. But all flights are now grounded until further notice, thank God, so he won't be able to kill himself in a plane just yet.

Yesterday I read a letter from a Danish Jew. The writer *named* someone who had his nails pulled out to make him give the names of his accomplices in illegal activity. In the course of this torture he betrayed various names including that of the letter-writer, who would now have to escape to Sweden. He also *named* several 80-year-old Jewish women who were pushed into the hold of a ship when they were being transported to Poland, so the fall would kill them. All those mentioned by name were evidently known to the recipient of the letter. The writer also claimed that 11-year-old Danish-Jewish girls had been taken to brothels in Germany.

All we can do is hope it isn't true.

I must be ravin' mad [quotation from the home help in Småland who exclaimed 'I must be ravin' mad, wearing red trousers when Olle's dead'], not writing a word about the Allies' conference in Moscow. It's been going on for quite a while. The British and American foreign ministers (Eden and Hull) are there. This is what everyone's interested in at the moment and there's great unease in Finland and other places about what might result.

It will soon be 11 November, Armistice Day, and Germany's in the grip of 11th November psychosis, one newspaper reported. The fact is that the whole world is waiting for the collapse of Germany, which really ought to come soon, given how bad things are on the eastern front. Yesterday I met a woman who'd been to Germany quite recently. People can't laugh there, she told me; their faces are grey and they seem to have given up entirely.

Badoglio has demanded Victor Emmanuel's abdication, I read the other day. I don't know if it's true, but it certainly seems unlikely that the house of Savoy will get through this war with its crown intact.

There are lots of stories going round about the king of Denmark. One story goes that when the Germans were planning to introduce the Star of David in Denmark, on the same model as in Germany, the king of Denmark said that in that case, he would be the first to wear it. And they never did bring in the Star of David. There's another story that when the Germans proposed to raise the swastika at Amalienborg, Christian said that a Danish soldier would instantly lower it again. 'Then that Danish soldier will be shot,' said the German commander-in-chief. 'I am that Danish soldier,' said the king.

The First World War ended 25 years ago today. Does anyone hold a minute's silence any more, like they used to between the wars? I don't think so. And all the little 'unknown soldiers' around the world, buried with such pomp and splendour, is there anybody who remembers them? Or are they forgotten on a day like today in favour of all the unknown soldiers confronted daily and hourly with [the realities of] life at the various fronts. Dear Lord Jesus, can't it be over soon?

I heard a dramatized documentary (one of Gierow's) on the radio this evening. It was called *1918 In Memoriam*. It made me so melancholy, 1918 was supposed to be the very, very last year of war in the history of mankind, but it wasn't to be. It was so sad to hear about all those who fell on the Somme and the Marne; their deaths were so utterly in vain; so completely unnecessary, since it was all going to happen again 25 years later.

On this Armistice Day there are reports in the paper of pogroms against the Italian Jews and other cheery topics. On this Armistice Day I had to take Lars to the eye specialist for the first time. I do hope he's not going to have bad eyes! On this Armistice Day Sture's got a committee meeting, and on this same day I am very sleepy, so I can't write any more. My kids are asleep in their beds.

29 NOVEMBER

Now we're into Advent, and can gradually start looking forward to Christmas. We snuggle up round the fire together and think how wonderful it is to have a home to be in, at least that's what I do. But I wonder how the Berliners feel about the prospect of Christmas. This week has seen the start of blanket-bombing of Berlin. District after district is being obliterated. It's too gruesome to think about. I don't like the British having to do this to win the war. Admittedly the Germans have already set an example with Warsaw, Rotterdam, Coventry and London, but it's just as ghastly when Berlin is the target, and one doesn't want the British behaving like the Germans. If only it was guaranteed that the bombs only fell on Nazis, but unfortunately they hit masses of innocent people, too. If one could just bundle together the Gestapo with all its murdering henchmen and bomb them to death, I wouldn't have an ounce of sympathy.

Sweden is pretty much flooded with refugees. We apparently have about 50,000 of them here. And we're drowning in refugees' post at work.

3 DECEMBER (FRIDAY EVENING)

This Friday evening 17 years ago I was lying there in labour, oww, the pain was terrible! It'll be nice to go to bed now and know one will at least probably sleep without pain. And tomorrow Lars will be 17. If he lived in Germany he would be, or would already have been, packed off on war service, not right to the front but even so.

The Germans have committed another truly wicked deed. On 30 November all Norwegian students were detained, to be sent to Germany. The Swedish government has complained in the strongest terms, but who knows with what result. The deportations apparently haven't happened yet. There's outrage in Sweden; the Swedish students are holding protests and demonstrations.

The bombing of Berlin goes on and on. Last night was terrible.

CHRISTMAS DAY

Sture, Karin and I went to Skansen [open-air museum and zoo](Lasse didn't want to come; he wanted to sleep) this Christmas morning, while Grandmother stayed at home to mind the house and ruined some oat biscuits in the oven. It's misty, autumnal weather, not a bit of snow, and the ground hasn't frozen to any depth, either. But our feet were freezing, Karin's and mine, though it was nice that there weren't many other people at Skansen; the great tits fluttered over to us and perched on our hands when we were trying to feed a shy little squirrel. There was a little deer running around free and that came up to sniff us as well.

Then we went home for some Christmas food, and now I'm sitting in front of the fire to write.

This is the fifth war winter – and we have more food than ever. In my refrigerator I've got two big hams, brawn, liver pâté and pork ribs, herring salad, two big pieces of cheese and some salt beef. Besides that, all my tins are full of home baking: ginger snaps, oat biscuits, brandy rings, almond fingers, gingerbread and meringues.

This is the second Christmas we've spent in Stockholm – and it all went off well again. This year, I'm pleased to say, Karin wasn't ill. She read the Christmas story from the Bible for us and played Father Christmas, too. The sack of presents was so heavy she could scarcely drag it in. Sture and I gave each other half a lamp = one whole one, with a blue pottery base and a natural-coloured silk shade. Apart from that the presents were for the children, of course: Lasse got a sports shirt, tie, woollen scarf, sport gloves, pants (2 prs), a puzzle, sweets, three books (*Red House, Chaffer K, Above Suspicion* – Helen MacInnes's), two rolls of film, money, brush and comb, slippers – and Karin got slippers, ice skates, a ski jacket, brush and comb, socks and mittens, a white jumper knitted by me, two paintboxes, the *Let's Sing Now* songbook,

Peter No-Tail's Great Escape, Mary Poppins Comes Back, Unforgettable Tales, money, sweets, etc.

Tomorrow the Frieses are coming round for a Christmas party and on the 27th Lars and Karin are off to Småland, with me following on New Year's Day.

I don't know a single person as fortunate as we are. Sture's getting a pay rise of 4,000 kronor a year from 1 January. And Mum and Dad gave us 1,000 kronor as a Christmas present again.

I really enjoyed getting things ready for Christmas here in our home, and all the while I felt a profound gratitude that this is still possible and that we live in such a peaceful part of the world. It sounds trite, but never mind, I feel so grateful that I can't put it into words – and am acutely aware that these must be the happiest years of my life, surely nobody can do as well as this in the long run? I'm fully expecting that trials will lie ahead. Everything's thrown into such sharp relief by the rest of the world being so full of misfortune and misery, such concentrated misery that when I heard the bright voices of a children's choir from Germany singing 'Stille Nacht' I went out into the kitchen and wept. Those children with their angelically lovely voices are growing up in a country where the whole idea is to do violence to other human beings. A book by a Czech author came out this autumn. It's called *The Dead Look On* [by Gerald Kersh] and is about the obliteration of the Czech village of Lidice after the murder of Heydrich. No one in the village had anything to do with the murder but the Germans wanted to make an example of them. So all the men over 16 were shot, after digging their own graves, all the women were sent as forced labour and all the children over three were taken away to some unknown destination in a lorry, in which 157 children were packed together in a space intended for half the number, so they had to stand the whole way. According to the book, the journey took seven hours, and several of the children were dead on arrival. I don't know how accurate the details in the book are, but if only half of them are true, the Germans have committed a bloody deed that will cry out to Heaven for all eternity. Then the whole village was blown up; within 24 hours, there was nothing left to indicate that the place had ever been a peaceful little village full of peaceful people.

And this is the work of the people who created 'Stille Nacht'. I came across this satirical version by Arnulf Øverland in one of my letters the other day:

> Silent night, holy night
> Dad's been nabbed, what a fright.
> No one can tell where they've shut him away.
> Nobody knows if he's in there to stay.
> Clothes on – don't hang about!
> They said as they bundled him out.
>
> Peace on earth, peace from above
> Child, beware your own brother's love.
> His traitor's kiss and your fate is foretold
> 'Winter Aid' is out in the cold.
> Wolves in sheep's clothing. Beware!
> They're with us everywhere.
>
> Yuletide peace, peace all around!
> Hear the guns' rattling sound!
> Deck the halls with paradise green
> The loveliest corpses that you've ever seen.
> Angelic voices sang
> even at Yang-tse Kiang!

The German battleship *Scharnhorst* was sunk up at the North Cape yesterday afternoon by British naval forces. There can't be much left of the German navy now.

> *[Press cuttings: picture of the* Duke of York, *which sank the* Scharnhorst, *unidentified source; lines from Hasse Zetterström's column in* Svenska Dagbladet, *29 December 1943, likening German treatment of some Danish children to Herod's behaviour, headed 'As for Christmas' by Astrid; long article 'The implication of Jewish persecution' by Hugo Valentin,* Dagens Nyheter, *28 December 1943.]*

1944

Astrid, Karin and Lars, 1943.

I don't seem to have had time to write anything since New Year. Nor did I cut out any of the 'reviews' of 1943 that were in the papers. But I'll stake my money on it being the 'year of peace' that has just dawned. There's *got* to be peace in 1944, and an end to this anarchy.

They announced the day before yesterday on 'Sveriges Radio', as it's to be known from the start of this year, that Kaj Munk, the clergyman and poet, was taken from his home in Vedersø, shot in the head with a pistol and then thrown in a roadside ditch. It's sad and upsetting enough to make you weep. The number of acts of violence in Denmark is growing from day to day; it seems worse there than anywhere else.

Reports came through the other day that the Russians have now reached the old Polish border, which has not been in their hands since the first week of the Germany–Russia war. Every communiqué speaks of German withdrawal to prepared positions and planned retreat – but only ever retreat and more retreat.

Now the children and I are at Näs. It hasn't been as lovely as last year, when the woods were like a fairy-tale forest with thick snow on every tree and bush – this year there's no snow at all. But it's been nice all the same, especially Twelfth Night when I had a couple of wonderful hours skating on the frozen Stångån [river] with Karin, Gunvor, Barbro and Karin Karlsson. I haven't spent much time with

Lars, he's had Göran for company, and anyway, we haven't been getting on very well; Lasse's very touchy these days. But things will improve. I hope!

Finnish authoress Hella Wuolijoki has been given a life sentence for spying for the Russians.

14 JANUARY

I was going to paste in a few things about the murder of Kaj Munk, which still shocks and upsets people, but I've mislaid the cuttings. So the best thing, while I still remember, is for me to try reconstructing the newspapers' version of events. So – Kaj Munk, who lived and worked in an insignificant little parish named Vedersø but whose words reached far beyond the borders of his parish and his country, had been out to some kind of little hunting lodge with his wife and children on that unfortunate day. When they got home and were having a meal, two, or it might have been three, uniformed men turned up, claiming to have an arrest warrant for Munk. He took a small bag, got in their car and was driven away – and was later found lying in a ditch, shot through the forehead. Today's papers say investigations revealed that those who did it were members of Frits Clausen's party.

In Italy the old Fascists who forced Mussolini out in July have been on trial and the verdicts are in. Most were sentenced to death, among them old Ciano, whose sentence has already been carried out. Ciano wanted to be shot from the front, with his eyes uncovered. According to yesterday's paper Edda Ciano, Mussolini's daughter, informed on her own husband. It all sounds like ancient Rome, if you ask me.

23 JANUARY

Since I last wrote there's been a big hoo-ha between Russia and Poland over their future borders; just as one would have expected, the Russians have proved unwilling to meet the Poles' demands.

In Russia they are now fighting it out for Leningrad; the Germans certainly seem to be surrounded there. In Italy, the battle for Rome is expected any day.

I'm sure other things have happened, too, but I don't recall them just now.

Oh yes, the Allies are nearing Rome.

And Argentina has broken with the Axis. The same Argentina which has been a long-standing and loyal Axis stronghold, but that's all over now. A letter to Axis 'agents' in Argentina was intercepted, but the Germans claim it's a forgery.

6 FEBRUARY

Nordahl Grieg, who was fighting with the free Norwegians based in Britain, has been killed.

Ten divisions of Germans are encircled at the Dnieper and at risk of annihilation. Their only links with their own side are by air. Their commanders flew to see Hitler and asked permission to capitulate, but Hitler said no. The Russians have now almost reached the Estonian border and the Estonians are fleeing in droves. To Finland and Sweden. Lots of them have been coming across to Gotland in small boats. Anything rather than fall into Russian hands.

At present we have around 40,000 refugees in Sweden. I'm not sure if I wrote about the 'police training' in the camps for the Norwegians. They call it that, but it's more like regular firearms training and military service. I gather from Norwegian refugee letters that they wear British army uniforms. I also saw it reported that they're being trained by British officers. One letter I saw, from Georg von Wendt, said Norwegians were being deported [from Norway] as a direct response to the weapons training being given to our Norwegian refugees. The deportation continues and Sweden does nothing, and presumably can do nothing, about it. But we made vocal protests about it in advance. The refugees here don't like us much, but perhaps that's only natural. It's dismal being a refugee, and easy to turn your frustration on your hosts. The Norwegians seem particularly resentful of us. I think I shall cut out an article by Aksel Sandemose in *Vecko-Journalen*. 'The people of France are starving and freezing', Célie Brunius wrote in *Svenska Dagbladet* today. Everything goes to Germany, as it does from all the other occupied countries. There's nothing to buy, no clothes, no shoes, no china, no food, nothing. In free France, it's even worse.

8 FEBRUARY

The day before yesterday, that is, when I last wrote, the evening news reported that about 200 Russian planes had carried out a bombing raid on Helsinki, inflicting great damage. This is believed to be the start of a campaign on the Russians' part to force the Finns into peace. There's very obvious alarm about the Russians now, in the letters and elsewhere.

Elsa Gullander told us yesterday that the Finland Aid Society rang to ask her if she could take Taina back. 'It might be nicer for you than compulsory billeting,' they said, and told her that Sweden is ready to take *800,000* Finnish refugees if things go catastrophically in Finland. All of Karelia is being evacuated again; what unspeakable misery for the Karelians, who returned to their land with such high hopes when the Russians were driven out. It's awful to contemplate the fate of Finland – and the poor Baltic states! Russian submarines have ventured out into the Baltic again, so our merchant vessels are back travelling in convoys. All the children and old people are being evacuated from Helsinki. I'm worried about the future – even here in Sweden, we will no doubt have heavy fates to bear, we can't expect everything to unfold in total peace here.

Peace, when it comes, might not be anything to rejoice about but just the opposite. By then, many of these poor little countries will have had to give up their freedom to live in eternal slavery.

17 FEBRUARY

The billboards tell us Helsinki is under violent Russian bombardment. And former minister Paasikivi is currently in Stockholm, dragged from the sanctity of private life to discuss peace with the Russians. That's what the whole world thinks, at least, though he doggedly insists he's here in a private capacity. But the idea of a Finland–Russia peace is currently in the air; it could even be 12 March again [as in 1940], who knows?

Berlin is still being pounded by bombs. I'm just reading *The World of Yesterday* by Stefan Zweig; it's a few years now since he, a refugee, took his own life somewhere in South America. He experienced two world wars and also the happy time before the First World War, when humanity's illusions were still intact. It's a sad book, especially as one always has the author's bitter fate at the back of one's mind and knows it is shared by countless other individuals, perhaps as warm-hearted as he seems to have been.

I have a quiet spell for my writing this evening. Sture's in Göteborg, Lars is doing his homework in his room and Karin has just been sick and gone to bed. She's going through some kind of nervous crisis, which expresses itself in exaggerated attachment to me and anxiety that something might happen to me. This concern only descends on her in the evenings. On Tuesday, Sture and I were off to dinner at the Viridéns, for Alli's 40th birthday, and when I came to say goodbye to Karin she said, 'You're saying farewell, as if you weren't coming back!' And when I got back, she had my dressing gown draped over her. I only hope it's just a phase.

Alli's dinner was a great success. The other guests were the Gullanders, Ingmans, Abrahamssons, Eveos and Palmgrens, plus the Hultstrands and a Miss Nyberg. Sigge took me in to dinner. I must write down what we had, partly because I enjoy writing about food and partly because one never knows, in times like these, how long we can carry on eating this way in Sweden. So: three cocktail sandwiches, mushroom croustade, asparagus soup with cheese straws, turkey with vegetables, ice cream and hot chocolate sauce. Sherry with the soup and dessert, red wine with the turkey. And then a little late-night supper: meatballs, mushroom omelette, herring salad and herrings au gratin. We danced and larked about and at 2 a.m. the people in the flat below called to complain, because by then we were dancing a polka fit to make the whole house shake. Enough of all that, I'm off to bed.

23 FEBRUARY

Yesterday evening when it was time for me to go down to work, Karin was afraid as usual that something might happen to me. I told her there was no need to worry; nothing would happen in our peaceful land. 'If we lived in a country at war, where there's bombing,' I said, 'that would be different.' So off I went to work, and on the 10 o'clock news they said that a short time earlier, unknown aircraft came in over Stockholm and dropped a load of bombs on Hammarbyhöjden, then flew on over

Södertälje and Strängnäs and dropped more there, too. There was no air-raid warning and no anti-aircraft fire (because the planes had sent out SOS signals). I'm grateful the bombs didn't fall here in Vasastan, because it would have done serious damage to Karin's nervous system. I kept the paper from her this morning, so she still doesn't know about it. The planes were Russian.

It's Karin and Lars's half-term holiday, though Karin only gets three days. Lars has gone on the school trip up to the fells at Enafors. Karin's been in bed with a cold part of the time but she and I also went out skiing. Today Elsa-Lena, Matte and their mums came round. The children were out on their skis. Some lovely sunshine.

3 MARCH

Well, as the article alongside shows, peace between Russia and Finland is on the cards. But Finland is dubious – and no wonder! – Norwegian and Danish refugees express their contempt of our terror of the Russians, but we know it's justified.

> *[Press cutting from* Dagens Nyheter, *1 March 1944: Moscow willing to receive Finnish delegation. Russia reveals its terms.]*

The translation opposite of a letter from a Latvian wife (smuggled out) to her husband in Portugal describes how it feels in Latvia (where they now have to put up with the Germans, after all).

> *[Typed transcript of a letter from Astrid's work at the censor's office.]*

And now the Russians are nearing their border. When the Germans collapse there'll be no hope for the Baltic states, as far as one can judge – and then, poor people.

Tage Bågstam told us poison has been distributed to the population so they can kill themselves if the worst comes to the worst. And I can't help feeling it will!

Either nothing much has been happening in the war or I've been too lazy to write anything. The most noteworthy thing at present is the peace negotiations between Finland and Russia. They've been going on for some time but without result, it seems. The Finns refuse to yield, despite pressure from Britain and the USA. The whole thing strikes me as rather mysterious. Finland's more or less got a knife to its throat and will surely *have to* agree to the Russians' conditions before long. King Gustaf apparently contacted Mannerheim and Ryti and appealed to them to try for a peace settlement.

On the home front, Karin's had a nasty case of the measles and still isn't allowed out of bed. I'm currently having really good fun with Pippi Longstocking.

I feel I've neglected to keep track of the Finnish–Russian peace negotiations as I ought; I don't think I've even said anything about Russia's conditions. They largely boil down (as far as one can tell) to the 1940 border and the internment of all German troops in Finland, with Russian help if need be. Finland's reply up to now has been 'no', they want the conditions more precisely defined first, but the Russians want them to surrender first and argue it out later.

Given the Finns' mistrust of Russia, no wonder the Finns want some guarantees first.

Lots of people are getting their call-up papers at the moment. Sture came home the other day and said the Germans plan to occupy Finland the same way they did Hungary, but I hope it isn't true. I'm so fed up with the war I can't bring myself to write about it. What's more, I'm in bed with a sprained foot. Bother!

On this day I have been married for 13 years. The beautiful bride is stuck in bed, however, which gets pretty boring in the long run. I like it in the mornings when they bring me tea and white bread with smoked ham in bed and I get the bed made for me and the place nicely tidied around me, but I loathe it at night, when I have to have some kind of hot compress on my foot and it itches like mad and Sture's asleep but I can't get off to sleep myself. I'm reading Maugham's *Of Human Bondage* and working on Pippi Longstocking.

It doesn't look as though there'll be peace in Finland. It's time for the children's programme on the radio, so I can't write any more for now.

It's possible that this diary contains a disproportionate amount about the Germans' rampages, because *Dagens Nyheter* is our daily paper and that's more anti-German than any other rag and never misses a chance of highlighting German atrocities. It's beyond all doubt, however, that such atrocities do actually happen. Even so, it says at the end of this cutting about Poland that the Poles 'would prefer the German regime' to the Russian 'if there were no other choice'. That's probably also the case in the Baltic states and other countries, but for that to appear in *Dagens Nyheter* must be a slip-up.

> *[Press cuttings from* Dagens Nyheter, *5 April 1944: 'Executions on the Streets of Warsaw'; 'Warsaw children in gangster leagues': children neglected, stealing guns; prices rocketing; segregated cinemas for Germans and Poles; 'Eminent Hungarians in concentration camps, others taken to Vienna as hostages'.]*

16 APRIL

The battle for Sebastopol, the final German stronghold in the Crimea, has started. The southern front looks precarious, I must say, the Russians are in Romania and will soon be threatening the German oil supply. They've also crossed the Czechoslovak border.

The Allies are cross with us and other neutral states for supplying things to Germany. And send us stern memos about it. But we don't care.

We marked Easter in our customary way. There's a lot of food in the land of Sweden, and I'll write down what we had, as guidance for future Easters. On Good Friday, completely untraditional calves' liver, on Easter Saturday, as usual, eggs and a smörgåsbord (home-made liver pâté, herring salad, marinated Baltic herring, cold poached Baltic herring, pickled herring, smoked reindeer, boiled ham with beetroot and I don't know what else) and ice cream for dessert. And Sture and I had a very posh sherry, because we were celebrating our wedding anniversary that day rather than on the 4th. On Easter Day we had roast chicken and on Easter Monday pork chops.

On Easter Saturday, Lasse claimed he had an invitation to a dance at some girl's place in Tureberg; I told him he was to be home by 1 o'clock. But he didn't get back till 4, I was beside myself and had rung round, waking everybody up, and discovered from Göran that he was at the Winter Palace with a girl called Britta-Kajsa Falk.

Karin's very nervy and I had my hands full with her over Easter. She's not much better now, either; I think it must be the after-effects of the measles, though she was pretty dotty even before that, of course. Since I'm tied to the flat thanks to my foot, she certainly can't be anxious on my account, but her mental state is terribly volatile, swinging from jittery high spirits to deep dejection and moaning about school and about having to play the piano. I'm feeling quite down myself at the moment, presumably because I haven't been able to go out for three weeks. And I hope to God that Karin will soon get better, because it's awful having her like this and I feel so sorry for her, too. Lasse's living it up and always seems to be invited out somewhere; can't settle when he's at home, either, it seems to me, which makes me very sad.

23 APRIL

On Saturday night Moscow Radio read out a declaration about the Finnish–Russian peace negotiations. It said that the Finnish response on 8 March was considered unsatisfactory and that Russia's conditions, which had been delivered to Paasikivi, represented its minimum demands. A Finnish delegation then went to Moscow and conferred with Molotov on 27–28 March. The following conditions were delivered to the delegation:

[Press cuttings from Svenska Dagbladet, *23 April 1944: list of seven conditions plus short accompanying piece, 'Sharp Russian declaration on the Finnish question'.]*

This blessed invasion that's been hanging in the air for several years now but never happens! There's talk of 'D-Day' and 'H-Hour', but nothing happens. Several different dates have been identified, but I reckon any invasion is going to be a long time coming. I think it's a war of nerves to keep the Germans tied up in the West.

> [*Press cutting from* Dagens Nyheter, *21 May 1944,
> captioned by Astrid 'The story of "Lili Marlene",
> the hit song of the Second World War'.*]

Although 'Lili Marlene' fever has abated now, I've included this cutting, because the tune will forever be linked with the Second World War, just as 'Tipperary' and 'Madelon' belong to the First.

I've also put in Ivar Harrie's review of *Der letzte Jude aus Polen* [*The Last Jew from Poland*, published as *The Promise Hitler Kept*] because it gives some idea of how the Germans ravaged that poor country. I don't doubt for a moment that this it's a true account; I've just been reading Norwid's book *Landet utan Quisling* [*The Land without Quisling*] (Poland) and the details of the atrocities tally. I don't think the Germans even bother to deny that the Jews have been exterminated.

> [*Unidentified press cutting. Review by Ivar Harrie of
> Stefan Szende's book* The Promise Hitler Kept.*]*

Karin was ten today, the fifth of her birthdays we have had to celebrate in wartime. Or rather, that's claiming too much; here at home we have peace, thank goodness, though it seems to have been touch and go this spring. The Allies disapproved strongly, and no doubt still do, of our export of ball bearings to Germany. But after all, the attack (which was perhaps feared) would have come from Germany; I don't understand what they'd gain by attacking us, but then nobody's asking me to.

To get back to Karin's birthday, we marked it in the usual way. Her presents included *Folkskolans läsebok* [*The Elementary School Reader*] in three parts, a Peter No-Tail book and the manuscript of 'Pippi Longstocking' in a smart black file. Also a swimsuit (seersucker), white canvas shoes with wooden soles, some blouse fabric, books from the Viridéns and Gullanders, plus money from Granny and Grandad and from Grandmother. She also had a new strap for her watch. Pelle [Viridén], Alli, Peter (Matte wasn't well) and Elsa-Lena came round for coffee and cake. It's been a cold, gusty day like nearly all the rest this spring; generally, summer arrives on Karin's birthday. Tomorrow we've got some girls from her class coming, which she's quite anxious about (what with being so nervy this term). She didn't want to invite them all but she's worried about what those she didn't will say.

Lasse's been in bed for the past fortnight with a 'pretty decent' bout of influenza, running a temperature that went up to 40°. He's supposedly better now but still has a cough. He wanted to go to the pictures last night, his first day out of bed, and there was a great slam-banging of doors when I wouldn't let him go despite persistent pestering on his part. But I expect he was a bit peeved after all that time stuck in bed.

6 JUNE

INVASION – finally! Allied troops, with support from the air, have landed in north-western France. Thousands of troop ships and thousands of planes crossed the Channel early this morning.

General Eisenhower addressed the occupied countries (we heard it too), as did King Haakon. Hitler has apparently made himself commander-in-chief of the German forces. This is a historic date and must surely be the prelude to an even bigger push. It'll be thrilling, just thrilling, to see how things go. The Allies have a huge advantage in both sea and air power.

Personally I've been in a foul mood this Swedish Flag Day and invasion day. Lasse came home yesterday with absolutely lousy final grades and will have to retake the year. And the place has been in a mess while I get ready for the trip to Vimmerby the day after tomorrow. Karin's exams are tomorrow.

The Allies have marched into Rome! And so, finally – the INVASION!

13 JUNE

For the past couple of days a Russian offensive has been under way on the Karelian Isthmus. The Russians clearly intend to force the Finns into subjugation now. The attack seems to have come quite unexpectedly and the Russians have broken through in several places and crossed the 1939 border. There'll be loads more Finnish children coming over here now.

The bridgehead in Normandy has deepened and widened in all directions. German resistance has hardened, but it still looks as if things are going the Allies' way. I can't keep up with operations in detail. On the news they were talking about Bayeux, Caen, Carentan and so on. Churchill went there on a visit and gave the V sign.

The kids and I are at Näs, enjoying our holiday in spite of really awful weather. It's poured and poured and *poured* with rain. But this afternoon it was quite warm and fair so Stina and I went for a lovely walk through Kohagen and down to the railway (passing a ditch that was simply full of Primula farinosa and we found a bird's nest at the edge), then down to Stångån [river], over the railway bridge, on to Nybble and then home. Nature really is in its finest raiment just now. Tonight Lasse had an evening out at Folkets Park with Stina and will very likely be home late. Karin's living a very happy and carefree life, not clinging to me at all. Tomorrow we're cycling to Målen. Karin got good marks as usual, including three Abs [pass with merit], I think it was.

MIDSUMMER DAY

This is more or less what's happened since last time. The Russian offensive on the Karelian Isthmus has continued unabated. Russian gains include Vyborg [Viipuri], alas and alack! Things look bad for the Finns. There's been a government crisis looming for a while. Tanner and Linkomies will have to go before there can be peace with Russia.

In Normandy, around 30,000 Germans are cut off on the Cherbourg peninsula, where they're holding their positions so far.

The Germans have come up with a new kind of devilry, namely robot planes, which fly in over England and cause explosions and huge fires. The British are highly indignant because the planes, being unmanned, can't be aimed at military targets and so cause indiscriminate damage.

Those are roughly speaking the most important things that have happened recently, I think.

And Lasse and I took ourselves off on a cycling trip: Virserum – Skirö – Holsbybrunn – Fagerhult – Kråkshult – Vimmerby. It was fine and warm both days and we dropped in on Mum and Dad in Holsbybrunn. And Småland was a delight, so beautiful.

Karin seems very good at falling off her bike and keeps grazing her legs.

Blood is spilt, people are maimed, misery and despair are everywhere. And I simply don't care. I'm only interested in my own problems. I always try to write a few words about what's been happening since my last entry. But now I can only write: a landslide has engulfed my existence and left me alone and shivering. I shall try to 'bide my time and wait for dawn', but what if no dawn comes?

I shall try to make myself write a little about what's happening in the world, anyway.

The Russians have made amazing gains and are already in the Baltic states, which the Germans certainly seem to propose giving up. The Russians are now extremely close to the East Prussian border. Things aren't going that fast in Normandy, but they are making progress there, too.

Representatives of the Finnish government went to see Ribbentrop and sealed the alliance with Germany still further. As a result, the USA has finally broken off diplomatic relations.

That's all I can remember. I'm in a state of agony, my heart aches so much – where will I find the strength to go back to town and pretend to live a normal life?

Alone at Dalagatan with bitter despair in my heart, Karin at Solö, Lasse in Näs, Linnéa on holiday, Sture?

There have been major developments, but I haven't felt like writing. Even something as remarkable as an attempt on Hitler's life hasn't stirred me into action.

And today it says in the paper that Finland's Ryti-Linkomies cabinet has stepped down. That is, Ryti was president, wasn't he? But now it's Mannerheim instead. The new government will try to get peace with Russia, of course.

'Turkey breaks with Germany,' the billboards say this evening. So things could all fall apart at any time.

Just as they have fallen apart for me.

23 AUGUST

Paris is liberated from the Germans. After four years' captivity. I remember the day we read on the billboards that the swastika was flying on the Eiffel Tower. That must be centuries ago.

27 AUGUST

The other day – the 23rd, I think – Romania surrendered and went so far as to declare war on Germany.

It seems inconceivable that Germany will hold out much longer. I found a good account of the war in the *Dagens Nyheter* Sunday supplement today. I'll paste it in, but first let me put in a gentleman who was on the 'Names in the News' page of *Dagens Nyheter* the other day.

[Press cutting from an undated article headed 'Culture Bus', with photo of Sture Lindgren, about how the Swedish motorists' association is planning for the end of the war.]

The original himself had gone astray. And I was sorely afflicted.

Today – this hot August Sunday – Ingvar, the children and I went to Skansen.

The war is just past its fifth birthday and everything's happening at once; it's such a shame I'm in no fit state to write much about it.

Finland has broken with Germany, and *a ceasefire with Russia has come into force*. (On 4 September, I think.)

Bulgaria has broken with Germany, too; and in fact declared war.

The first German cities have been taken by the Allies.

The Russians are on the march through Eastern Pomerania. It can't be long before the Germans give up.

This evening's papers say it's war between Finland and Germany. German naval forces attempted to land at various points last night. Peace negotiations between Russia and Finland are in full swing.

[Short, unidentified, incomplete press cutting about Europe marching on Germany.]

I make entries in here more and more rarely. I've got so much else to think about and I've been in such a state of nervous tension all autumn that I couldn't bring myself to write anything. Just at the moment it looks as though the worst crisis might be over, but I can't really be sure yet whether things are going in the right direction. But there are a few cheering things happening as well.

> *[Unidentified cutting: 'Secondary-school teacher wins first prize in girls' book competition'. Astrid Lindgren has won the second prize in the competition, run by children's book publisher Rabén & Sjögren, for a book which the article says will probably be called 'The Confidences of Britt'.]*

Incidentally, the Russians are fighting in Northern Norway and it looks as though they can forget Finnish independence.

Letter from a German officer to his Swedish wife. He was killed just afterwards.

> *[Typed transcript of a letter from Astrid's work at the censor's office. The writer is in a dugout under fire. He suggests a boy's and a girl's name for the child she is expecting.]*

> *[Photograph from Vi magazine of Astrid's brother-in-law and sister with an old man. Lindgren has copied out the text.]*

A Vimmerby resident currently known across the land is the young author and journalist Hans Håkansson, who has made a name for himself with his novels about stonecutters in Småland and his other stylistically and psychologically well-written books. This year he changed his name and is now known as Hans Hergin. Here we see Hans Hergin and his wife Stina on their way to Vimmerby market, arm in arm with the town's toughest old boy, 92-year-old Johan Petter Svensson, rarely called anything but 'Lucke'.

My very first review.

> [*Press cutting from* Stockholms-Tidningen, *23 November*
> *1944: 'Prizewinning books' includes a positive review of her*
> Britt-Mari lättar sitt hjärta *(The Confidences of Britt-Mari).]*

26 NOVEMBER

On this dark November Sunday I'm writing in front of the fire in the living room while Lasse is getting dressed – it's 3.30 – and Karin's in her room, typing (no, she just came to join me!) Sture is not home, far from it. Karin and I went for a walk to Haga cemetery this afternoon.

Other than that, the world looks roughly like this: there's appalling misery among the civilian population in Northern Norway, who have been forced to evacuate in the face of the Russian advance. There's terrible hardship in Holland too, in fact where isn't there terrible hardship? It seems to be everywhere. In West Germany it's ghastly, with the persistent bombing, and what's more the Allies are now on German soil.

Hitler is saying absolutely nothing, to the whole world's amazement. The Nazis had some kind of jubilee recently and Hitler didn't speak at that either, but Himmler gave an address and said Hitler had so much to do at headquarters that he hadn't got time to make a speech to the people. And the people, dreading the sixth winter of the war, could certainly have done with a word from their Führer.

The Gotland ferry the *Hansa* went down a few nights ago on the way from Nynäshamn to Visby. Presumably it was torpedoed. Two were rescued but about 100 people went down with the ship. It's the worst disaster to befall Sweden in modern times.

The Germans announced a while ago that the whole Baltic outside territorial waters was to be viewed as a war zone. Sweden protested. This is probably their response to our protest, I imagine.

17 DECEMBER

How about writing something in this little book? I'm sitting alone in front of the fire this third Sunday in Advent. Lasse's at the pictures, Karin round at Matte's making 'Christmas tree baskets'. Sture's in Göteborg, unless he's back by now. In exactly a week's time it will be Christmas Eve, and yesterday a hamper arrived from Vimmerby bringing ham, salt beef, pig's liver, shoulder of pork and more besides, so we won't starve during the abattoir-workers' strike.

It doesn't look as if there'll be peace just yet. German resistance in the West has intensified, and in spite of the terrible bombing it seems their will to go on fighting can't be crushed that easily. The Russians are pushing forward: Budapest is clearly being razed to the ground. In Greece, revolutionary troops have been fighting back against the British invasion corps and the puppet government; the Russians are probably behind it. In Northern Norway only an invasion can save hundreds of thousands from starving to death, it said in the paper the other day. There's such horrific and desperate need all over Europe that one simply can't take it in. Except here! The sixth Christmas of the war will be celebrated as usual. How the celebrations will go in the Lindgren family is perhaps a bit more problematic. But I hope things will go well. Meanwhile, I'm really pleased about 'Britt-Mari'.

'I am acutely aware that these must be the happiest years of my life, surely nobody can do as well as this in the long run? I'm fully expecting that trials will lie ahead.' That was what I wrote last Christmas Day. I didn't know how right I was. Trials *did* lie ahead – but I still wouldn't say I'm unhappy. I've had a hell of a six months this second half of 1944 and the ground beneath me has been shaken to its very foundations; I'm disconsolate, down, disappointed, often melancholy – but I'm not really unhappy. There's still so much to fill my existence. By any standards it should have been an awful Christmas – and it's true I shed some bitter tears into the herring salad when I was making it on the 23rd, but I was so exhausted at that point that it doesn't count. And besides, if happy is synonymous with being fortunate, then I suppose I'm still 'happy'. But being happy isn't that simple. There's one thing I've learnt – if you're to be happy, it has to come from inside you and not from another person. In spite of everything, I think I've done pretty well at finding things to be happy about. But I have a feeling I may be put under even more pressure and then we'll see how clever I am.

Anyway, I've managed to have Christmas here at home without the children or Grandmother noticing anything but peace and happiness, I think. Both the children were so pleased with their presents and their Christmas Eve.

Lasse had: anorak, ski boots, cardigan, white woollen scarf, two pairs underpants (he gets those every year), cufflinks, everyday trousers, a new watchstrap, *All the Adventures in the World*, [Helen MacInnes's] *While We Still Live*, a marzipan pig; those were the ones I bought, and he got other presents from Karin and Ingegerd and visiting cards from the Lagerblads and money from Granny and Grandad. Karin had a pleated grey skirt, dark-blue cardigan, socks, *The Black Brothers* and *Shipwreck*

Island [stories by German-born Swiss writer Lisa Tetzner], *Swedish Plants, Gustav Vasa's Adventures in Dalarna* [children's history book by Anna Maria Roos], copies of *The Fairytale Prince* and *The Fairytale Princess* [story magazines], Happy Families, a puzzle, a marzipan pig, a purse, plus *Mary Poppins Opens the Door* from Matte, writing paper from Ingegerd, a puzzle from Linnéa, money from Granny and Grandad. I had a very nice alarm clock from Sture, which was delivered a few days before Christmas Eve. Karin was delighted to be giving me a bath brush.

We forgot to dip bread in the ham stock [a seasonal Swedish custom] on Christmas Eve – but otherwise everything followed the usual regulations.

This morning Lasse and I took a walk out towards Haga. Sture didn't want to go to Skansen this Christmas Day, oh no, you bet he didn't!

This afternoon I roasted a goose and braised some red cabbage – and made a batch of apple sauce, a strange occupation for Christmas Day, but the apples wanted using up. On the 27th the children are off to Småland – and I shall follow on New Year's Eve and oh, how I'm longing for that! I shall be on sick leave for three weeks, for 'neurosis and insomnia'.

If all were as it should be, it would be just *too* good! What with Britt-Mari and everything! But now all is not as it should be, and perhaps that's the whole point! What's more, one only has to look about one in the world a little to appreciate that nothing is as it should be, nor will ever be.

Well I'm blowed, the Germans have mounted an *offensive* in the West. This war isn't going to end for some time yet, not by any means!

1945

Anne-Marie Fries, Astrid, and their colleague at the censor's office, Birgit Skogman. Lidingö, 1945.

I've shamefully neglected to write anything of late. But there's been plenty going on, all the same. The German offensive in the Ardennes has been repelled; a whole lot of Russian offensives are in progress, including in Poland, where Warsaw, according to the evening papers today, has been liberated from the Germans. There's been protracted and violent fighting around Budapest. There can't be much left of the city, I should imagine. *Dagens Nyheter* is running a series of articles under the title 'On the Threshold of Peace', so they evidently think it can't go on that much longer, after all. Down at work they're starting to worry about their jobs – I'm still off sick, and as things stand, everything looks so gloomy. However hard I scan the future, everything looks dark – yet Sture insists all that's in the past. *He who lives will see* [in English].

The Russians are storming ahead. What if they reach Berlin! It might be best if I cut out the bulletins every day, as these clashes could be the crucial ones.

Crucial clashes are in progress between Sture and me, too, and it's a long time since I've felt as downhearted as I have these past few days.

The Allies are advancing on the western front. Cologne is under artillery fire. The Russians are moving forward on the eastern front, though not as fast as might have been expected a while back – it doesn't look as if they'll be in Berlin tomorrow, exactly. There has been a terrific series of bombing raids on Berlin recently and it's a sheer miracle Germany's still holding together. Turkey has declared war on Germany at the eleventh hour – to secure a place for itself at the meeting in San Francisco.

My own private war seems to have about ended, too – in victory for me.

Other than that, I'm busy writing 'Barbro and I' [published as *Kerstin and I*] – that's the most enjoyable thing I have at the moment.

Grandmother is 80 today. We're not there but we have sent her cake, chocolate, a book and some glassware. It's now the vernal equinox of 1945. And today, spring is in the air.

We've had dinner (a very nice one of roast reindeer, smoked prawns, liver pâté, roast beef)! Sture's taking an after-dinner nap. Karin is translating from Danish, Lasse's playing the banjo guitar and I'm writing.

I've no newspaper cuttings to hand, so I'd better try writing a little from memory.

In Finland, things have been coming to a head of late. At the start of March their minister of labour Wuori gave a remarkable radio address, basically saying that all traces of Nazism would have to be eradicated from Finland or the country would suffer for it. The parliamentary elections, wider in scope than any before, ended in victory for the 'democrats', that is, the Communists, who have been banned in Finland since 1930 but now have the wind in their sails.

Germany is being completely wiped out. There soon won't be a German soldier west of the Rhine. There was an upsetting description in *Stockholms-Tidningen* the other day about the state of things in Germany – I haven't got it, unfortunately. Hitler doesn't want to surrender; he's worried history will deliver a shameful verdict, that was one thing the article said.

As for the Lindgren family, I can say 'Home is the sailor, home from the sea, and the hunter home from the hill' [in English].

Here, everything's spick and span after all the spring-cleaning, and sometimes I'm happy and sometimes I'm sad. I'm happiest when I'm writing. I had an offer from [the publisher] Gebers a couple of days ago.

I forgot to say that the Shell Building, the German headquarters in Copenhagen, was levelled to the ground by Allied bombers. A Catholic school caught fire and lots of children were killed.

Norway has seen many executions by firing squad.

26 MARCH

Yesterday, Sunday afternoon, Churchill went by landing craft across the Rhine to the American Ninth Army's bridgehead.

6 APRIL

Easter is over – Sture and I spent it here on our own, and the children were in Småland – and it's all been quite intense. Historic days as Germany gradually crumbles, surely the last weekend before its collapse.

> *[Unidentified short press cuttings: latest from the fronts;*
> *a Finnish coalition government is formed; two Danes*
> *summarily executed by the Germans; Roosevelt's funeral.]*

14 APRIL

Via the Red Cross, Sweden has sent food supplies to the starving in Holland. Here is a letter of thanks to the king and the Swedish people.

> *[Press cutting from* Dagens Nyheter, *14 April 1945:*
> *letter from a Miss Koens and a Miss Kardinaal in*
> *Amsterdam to 'Sire and the Swedish people'.]*

25 APRIL

Berlin is a smoking heap of rubble, and according to the evening news a little while ago completely surrounded by the Russians.

It takes me several hours to cut everything out of the papers. The evening papers excel in gruesome descriptions of the concentration camps in Germany. I don't want to put them all in.

To me it feels as if there's a smell of fresh blood emanating from Germany, and a terrible sense of doom. It feels like *Untergang des Abendlandes* [the fall of the West].

German women have been taken to see the horrors of Buchenwald – as have a number of neutral press reporters.

I've read lots of letters from Danish Jews, whom the Red Cross brought back from Theresienstadt. They are now very happily housed in a camp near Strängnäs. The Red Cross also brought Swedish and Norwegian students home, but that's all top-secret for the time being. The Jews' letters were deeply moving. Even though Theresienstadt was a *comparatively* decent place and the Danes had special status.

The San Francisco conference started today (without any Roosevelt). Just *imagine* all the half-baked theories they'll put forward!

> *[Under Astrid's heading 'Geschichten aus dem Buchenwald' (Stories*
> *from Buchenwald), a press cutting from Svenska Dagbladet,*
> *26 April 1945: 'Terrible instruments of torture and destruction'.*
> *'Astonishing will to live among many of the prisoners'.]*

29 APRIL

This Sunday morning, when we were woken by the sound of the rain gushing in the gutters, the huge headline in the paper read:
THE GERMANS SURRENDER!
Germany surrenders – finally! Why not earlier, before the whole of Germany was reduced to a pile of rubble and so many children aged 10–12 were sent to their deaths?

We heard it first on last night's news. Sture and I were sitting there, having our usual little Saturday powwow, but there have been so many rumours going round lately that one hesitates to believe anything in a hurry.

Himmler, that monster, proposed the peace and claims Hitler's dying and won't survive the surrender by more than 48 hours.

The whole thing's been mediated by a Swede – Count Folke Bernadotte, head of the Swedish Red Cross. Unconditional surrender – no wonder Hitler's dying. Perhaps he's been dead for ages, perhaps Himmler had him killed. Just think, the war's coming to an end, it's unimaginable! Germany lost it after Stalingrad, really – why did the pointless fight have to go on for so many years?

In parliament the other day there was a secret plenary to take a decision on possible armed intervention in Norway. They voted almost unanimously *against*. Quite right, why should we enter the fray at the eleventh hour? Luckily the question is now immaterial, because both Norway and Denmark will very probably be given up without a fight – Allied condition. And I can't believe the Germans in Norway are so crazy that they'll keep up the fight on their own.

But all the youngsters, the Norwegian refugees, and Danes too, who are here in our country preparing to go back home and do their bit in the final struggle, might be disappointed. The Norwegian government in London is (or was) disappointed in us for not wanting to get involved. It's not the first time they've been disappointed in us for one thing or another, but I reckon we can take it with equanimity. Think how disappointed the British and French were when we wouldn't join in the punch-up in Finland and let Allied troops through to fight Russia, which at that time was allied with Germany. *What* would the world look like now if we'd been swayed by their disappointment! Germany and Russia united, dear oh dear, then Britain would have been in a real fix. And how let down they felt when we, having very little choice, were obliged to let the German leave trains through to Norway, which certainly was a deplorable and painful episode, but the most sensible course of action in the long run. Because Sweden was needed outside the war. Looking back, we've achieved a fair bit, nothing to get all puffed up about of course, but gratifying all the same. We provided unprecedented material aid to Finland. And almost as much to Norway. We've been a place of refuge for nearing – what shall I say – 100,000 Norwegian and Danish refugees, perhaps that's a slight overestimate, I'm not sure. We've run courses for them in special 'police camps' that provided little short of standard military training. And now, in these last days, we were able to arrange for the Danes and Norwegians interned in Germany, Jews and others, to be brought to Sweden. I've read some of the letters that these young people sent to their families at home once they got here, and they're exultant. 'Think that life can be so glorious' – 'Are we dreaming?' and so on. It's the joy of being able to sleep in a proper bed, eat proper food, walk in the forest to pick wood anemones and live a normal life, in spite of everything. One wrote that he had God to thank above all, and then the Swedish Red Cross. And now we have a Swede acting as intermediary to bring the peace offer from Germany. *Somebody's* got to stay neutral, otherwise there can never be peace – for want of intermediaries.

Just think that there's to be peace! It'll be May in a few days' time – it's spring, the trees are turning green and the lovely rain is falling on the land that will now have to yield enormous harvests to keep the human race alive. There won't be another wartime winter, thank God! I'm glad the war's ending in spring, so that poor, tormented peoples have time to get ready, rebuild a bit and lay in some food, before winter comes again.

Spring 1945 – we never thought it would go on so long.

EVENING

It was a lie! The surrender. But it's going to happen in the next few days, at any rate. Somebody in America let the cat out of the bag. The part about Folke Bernadotte bringing a verbal message from Himmler was true. But I expect they are only willing to surrender to Britons and Americans, not to Russians. And Stalin doesn't want to agree to any surrender until the German army has been completely crushed. There are so many rumours buzzing about that it's hard to know what to believe. There are confident claims that Hitler died of a stroke at the start of the week, but it might not be true. According to today's papers, Mussolini's been shot.

A little while ago we had the Lund students on the radio, serenading the spring: 'O, hur härligt majsol ler' ['How the glorious may sun smiles'] and 'Blommande sköna dalar' ['Valleys in beautiful bloom'] and all the rest. Before that we had chicken and sherry and cheese; the sherry was in honour of today's big news – Denmark is free, the Germans are shoving off. (That wasn't quite the truth!)

Sture and Karin and I went to Skansen this morning, and it was spring there; we sat in the sun outside Älvrosgården and caught the scent of spring. Yesterday it was cold and rainy but today, spring's here. A very special spring, not just any old spring but the spring when peace came at last. Goodness gracious, how wonderful it is!

This afternoon I typed up a couple of chapters of 'Barbro and I', or whatever it's going to be called, if it ever gets into print.

Right, time for [the news from] TT: Count Bernadotte said at a press conference that around 15,000 internees were brought home to Sweden from the camps in Germany.

But he has no peace offer with him this time. He said he is convinced that Hitler – dead or alive – is in Berlin.

At this very moment the surging tones of 'Deutschland, Deutschland über alles' are pouring from my radio. A moment ago, the usual programme was interrupted for an extraordinarily important announcement. At 21.26, a *Meldung für das deutsche Volk* [message to the German people] was transmitted from Hamburg. *Unser Führer* Adolf Hitler died this afternoon, fighting Bolshevism to the last. Grand Admiral Dönitz has been appointed his successor. *The battle will go on.* Then Dönitz addressed the German people, and the national anthem followed. And even though Hitler and Nazism are the very quintessence of horror, the fall of a major country inevitably makes a deep impression on us as it crashes down into the abyss. Now they're repeating the broadcast from Hamburg, I can hear Dönitz saying *Schenckt mir Euren Vertrauen* [Give me your trust]!

This is a historic moment. Hitler's dead. Hitler is dead. Mussolini's dead, too. Hitler died in his capital, in the ruins of his capital, amid the ruins and rubble of his country.

'The Leader fell at his post of command,' Dönitz said.

Sic transit gloria mundi!

5 MAY

Rejoice, rejoice! Denmark is free again, after five years of serfdom. Holland too. Surrender at 7 o'clock this morning. When I was walking to work this morning and suddenly saw all the Danish, Swedish and Norwegian flags, I couldn't help the tears coming to my eyes.

At work we listened to King Christian's speech to 'Danish men and women' at 11 a.m. He was introduced by the chimes of the clock at Raadhustornet [the tower of City Hall], and after his speech they sang 'Kong Christian Stod ved Højen Mast' [the Danish royal anthem], for which we all stood up. The sun is shining on this, Denmark's day of freedom.

The papers are full of news – I don't know how I'll keep up with cutting it all out. They devote a lot of space to all the Danish and Norwegian (and other) prisoners brought to Sweden by the Swedish Red Cross.

I'm scribbling this down in a hurry in my lunch break.

5 MAY, 7-SOMETHING IN THE EVENING

Sven Jerring is in Copenhagen right now, and on the radio I can hear Danes of both sexes going wild with jubilation.

7 MAY

It's VE Day! The war's over! The war's over! THE WAR IS OVER!

At 2.41 p.m. (I think), the surrender was signed in a little red schoolhouse in Reims, for the Allies by Eisenhower (Bedell Smith), for the Germans by Jodl, under the terms of which all German forces in the whole of Europe capitulated. Norway's free now, too. At this very moment, a wild sense of jubilation is spreading across Stockholm. Kungsgatan is ankle-deep in paper and everyone seems to have gone crazy. We sang 'Ja, Vi Elsker' [the Norwegian national anthem] at work after the radio broadcast at 3 o'clock. Sture isn't in for dinner this evening, but he sent home a bottle of sherry so we could celebrate the peace. They're playing 'The Star-Spangled Banner' on the radio at the moment. I've been drinking sherry with Linnéa and Lars and feel a bit giddy. It's spring and the sun is shining on this blessed day and the war is over. I wouldn't want to be German. Just think, the war's over, Hitler's dead (there's shouting and cheering on the radio now;

Stockholm has completely taken leave of its senses). 'The waves of joy are still washing over Kungsgatan,' the announcer is saying, 'It's a gloriously wonderful day.'

I slipped Lasse an extra two kronor and he went dashing off to join the crowds all over the world. I gave Karin one krona and she celebrated the peace by buying sweets.

A Norwegian woman has just come on, and she's talking about how she felt when peace arrived: she's longing to see her son, who is in England.

Oh, oh, now it's over, all the torture and concentration camps and bombing raids and *Ausradierung* [eradication] of cities, and perhaps battered humanity can have a little rest.

Germany and the Germans are hated – but one can't hate *all* Germans, one can only pity them.

The war is over – it's the only thing that matters at the moment.

The war is over! The official announcement will be made from Great Britain, America and Russia simultaneously.

Alli and I and Karin and Matte took a tram down into town to see with our own eyes what Stockholm looked like on this historic day and struggled our way along Kungsgatan through the excited crowds. Then we took the tram home – and I've just heard on the evening news how overjoyed they are in Norway. A crowd gathered outside Møllergata 19 [the Nazi headquarters in Oslo], that ill-famed address, and sang the national anthem to the prisoners, though some have already been released. King Gustaf addressed the Swedish people from Drottningholm Palace; he's sent a telegram to Haakon. With the surrender came a severing of diplomatic ties with Germany. We saw three policemen outside the German tourist office in Kungsgatan as we walked past, and there was a cover over the window. After all the German arrogance proclaimed from there! And I've lost count of the number of times the windows were smashed during the war! There can be nothing more bitter than being German – when other countries were defeated by Germany, they could at least take a little comfort from the sympathy shown them by other nations. But now that Germany lies defeated, the whole world is rejoicing. How is it possible for a country to become so hated, why did they commit such bestial deeds and pose such a threat to all humanity?

(I had a glass of sherry with Esse, too. He's definitely intending to go back to Denmark.)

Tomorrow Churchill will speak, and Stalin and Truman, and the king of England!

8 MAY, 2.15

It's one historic moment after another. I just heard Winston Churchill inform the world of the unconditional surrender of all German forces in Europe and announce that we can finally celebrate VE Day, Victory in Europe Day. He made the announcement with the radio microphone used by Chamberlain to declare war on Germany in September 1939.

Good old Winston, he's really the one who won the war.

Hostilities will end at one minute after midnight on Thursday 8 May, Churchill said. How must it feel to that vigorous old man of over 70 to announce that to the British empire? He spoke like a man in his prime, in resounding tones, and I liked him more than ever. Then they played 'God Save the King' and its surging majesty almost made me cry.

I'm off work sick today, as luck would have it. Sture rang me last night from the Strand [hotel and restaurant] at 10 o'clock, and again at 11, and wanted me to come out and celebrate victory, but I was too tired, and he said he'd be home in an hour. He got back at 3 o'clock, in a delicate and happy state, and by then I was half out of my mind with worry, stupidly enough. And not being able to sleep for most of the night gave me a headache, so I'm at home and can listen to Churchill. Things must have been pretty lively in the restaurants of Stockholm last night. In the [Strand's] back restaurant all the diners sang and recited and did their party pieces. There's no mistaking the delight at the peace here!

9 O'CLOCK IN THE EVENING

I just heard the king of England address his empire. He spoke better than I expected, slowly and with only a couple of slight stammers. I'll paste his speech in here in due course.

Earlier today I heard Crown Prince Olav, King Haakon and Prime Minister Nygaardsvold. And now VE Day is coming to a close and I can't keep myself awake until a minute past twelve, when the cannons fall silent. In fact, they already have; to save human lives, I think they sounded 'cease fire' yesterday.

WHIT MONDAY

Written in the sunshine by the window on Karin's birthday. Beautiful Whitsun weather but lethargic family, refused to go out this morning. I sat on my own by a flowering bird cherry in Vasa Park. And longed for the countryside. First thing this morning we presented Karin with a cake, a briefcase, a fountain pen, books and some skirt material. We're about to have dinner, chicken and cake. The sailor [in English] is home, but he's been out sailing quite a lot lately. I finish my 'sordid job' [at the censor's office] on 1 July. I shall miss the company of my colleagues – and the income. But now the war's over, and there's no need for state security any more. Though things don't exactly seem quiet, if you ask me. The San Francisco conference isn't getting anywhere and the Russians have made new demands. The Poland question is causing problems and the Russians have occupied Bornholm, which I doubt they'll let go of, so that will give them mastery of the whole Baltic Sea.

I'm scared of the Russians.

[Typed transcript of Norwegian letters from Astrid's work at the censor's office: a female and a male testimony of their time when held prisoner at Møllergata and in the concentration camps.]

[Press cutting from Dagens Nyheter, *19 May 1945: 'Dying Berlin terrorized by the SS and other criminals'.]*

2 JUNE

I haven't been following daily events very closely over the past week, but there's trouble in the Levant and de Gaulle is furious and Marshal Tedder of the Royal Air Force was over here and in Norway and the refugees are going back home and we've been given notice from our 'secret' jobs from 1 July, so peace seems to have broken out in earnest, though one can scarcely believe it with the victors still squabbling the way they are. Russia is holding on to Bornholm.

I sold 'Barbro and I' (if that's what they call it) and got 800 kronor for it, and the rest of *Britt-Mari* brought in 300 kronor and the Finnish translation just over 300 kronor and they gave me 58 kronor for a reading of *Britt-Mari* on the radio. I do so enjoy being an 'author'. At the moment I'm reworking 'Pippi Longstocking' to see if I can make anything of that bad child.

It's a cold start to the summer and I feel rather on edge at times, yet at others I'm in high spirits. It's going to be sad parting from my colleagues at work. I've been sleeping rather badly lately. On Thursday, Karin sits her entrance exam for the grammar school. Lars is often out at student parties and he's got this wild notion of going to England as a deckhand on a ship. Sture has meetings almost every evening.

17 JUNE

World politics has had to take care of itself for a while, there hasn't been time to pay attention. Karin's now *taken* her entrance exam and got a place at the grammar school at Sveaplan, thank goodness, as has Matte.

Lars *has* signed articles, as a deckhand on the *Ardennia*, which is on its way to Rotterdam via Sundsvall, and I think about him a lot and wonder how he'll get on. Karin got simply splendid grades and Lasse failed three subjects, poor chap; I do wonder how things will turn out for him!

Sture has made another comeback, or so it seems.

And King Haakon and Crown Princess Märtha are back in Norway. King Leopold would like to go home to Belgium, but it seems the Belgian people don't want him. I'm sure various other things have happened, but I can't bring them to mind at the moment. Here we sit, Sture and I, with our children spread to the four winds, and in the evenings I really miss them.

It's perishing-cold most of the time, with wind and rain, ugh! Yesterday Sture and I went to the pictures to see *Dodsworth*, an old film that Sture couldn't abide.

I don't think we've ever had such lovely weather for midsummer; after a terrifically raw and chilly start to the summer the warm weather's arrived just in time for the holiday. But it could vanish again just as fast.

Sture and I are spending midsummer on our own at Dalagatan, a very sensitive midsummer and a bit wet. We're about to have chicken and then we're off to the veranda at the Strand for coffee and liqueur, and then the Kar de Mumma revue at the Blanche [theatre]. This morning, once I'd cleaned the flat, I cycled out to Haga on my own, while Sture stayed at home to read the paper. I sat in the sun above Mor på Höjden [café] and almost melted.

I hope Karin enjoys her midsummer at Solö. Lasse's in Sundsvall; he rang me the night before last. He'll go to Göteborg first, then on to England and Holland. It was nice being able to talk to him for a while.

Yesterday Sture and I went to see a rerun of *You Can't Take It with You*, an old Capra film.

I've finished revising Pippi and now I'm meant to be starting on a new, more normal children's book. But Per-Martin has suggested trying to write a new family series for the radio. It would be great fun if I could pull it off. I'm afraid it'll turn out to be a load of rubbish, though.

My job at the censor's office ends in a week – and then we're off to the country.

18 JULY

It's too hot to write. Though Churchill and Truman are in Berlin on a sightseeing tour of Hitler's Reich Chancellery and other more prominent landmarks, those that have survived. Stalin is also on his way there. Apart from that I don't know what's going on in the world. In Japan the fighting is still in full swing.

We're fighting in Furusund, too. With Grandmother. About ham, among other things. This heatwave is just insane and we're gasping like fish washed up on dry land. Sture, Karin and I are here. We've come full circle since 7 July last year.

Lars is being rocked on the ocean waves, I know not where. I think about him every night and regret letting him go. He ought to be back by now.

The censor's job ended on 31 June. The evening before, we had a farewell party at Bellmansro [restaurant]. There was a marvellous atmosphere and we enjoyed ourselves. The day after, the last day at work, felt rather sad and there were tears in some quarters. We had lunch at the Victoria, Anne-Marie and Rut Nilsson and I, Miss Nygren and Rydick, Dubois, Skyllerstedt and Wikberg. Nirsch came along for a while as well. And afterwards we all bade each other a tender farewell in Kungsträdgården [park]. It was the end of an era.

I'm keeping a slightly daft diary here in Furusund between the downpours. This evening Linnéa and I are going over on our bikes to fetch Matte.

If only I had Lars back home again!

15 AUGUST

Today the Second World War ended. Cessation of hostilities between Japan and the Allies, they announced on the news this morning. We heard Attlee speak and then they played the British, American, Russian and Chinese national anthems. Before all that, Swedish listeners heard Eyvind Johnson talking about peace.

Imagine it finally ending at last. Six years, give or take two weeks. How well I remember sitting in Vasa Park when Alli came up and said the Germans had marched into Poland. That was a fine, warm day, and it's ended on a fine, warm day as well. I celebrated the peace by helping with the oats on Slätö. It was *hot* and the sun was shining. Karin and Gunvor took the poles round in the cart and helped us put the sheaves in stooks as well. So did Stina.

Sture had an operation, his appendix, and I was in Stockholm with him for a fortnight, rather than in Småland. Now I've a week left before school starts again. Lars is home from his trip abroad and is at Norra Latin's summer hostel catching up on some revision. Summer will soon be over.

Oh yes, I forgot – Marshal Pétain was condemned to death yesterday evening. But in view of his age, the sentence probably won't be carried out.

I wonder whether things really are calm all round the globe at this moment, whether there are no bombs falling, no cannons firing, no warships sinking, and how quiet and strange it would be if that were so!

[Press cutting: 'Englishmen drive more slowly than we do'. Unidentified short article about recent visit to London by Sture Lindgren in his capacity as head of the Swedish motorists' association. Comments on slow speed of driving and the heavy London traffic.]

20 NOVEMBER

The English drive more slowly than we do and Pippi Longstocking is funny – with these idyllic observations I shall round off today's crop of cuttings, a change from the horrors they normally deal with. I sat here all evening pasting in cuttings from the past month's papers and more; it's been such a long time since I last wrote anything. Plenty has happened, as I hope the cuttings show. Unfortunately I didn't save anything about the execution of Quisling,* which was carried out one day, or rather one night, in October, when he was brought from prison in a police car to Akershus [Fortress], where he was shot. One gets the feeling the fellow really believed he had done his best for Norway – remarkably enough. Be that as it may, he's now feeding the worms. Just like Laval. And soon it'll be the big German villains, who go on trial today. Every country is having a good purge at the moment. And picking out its scapegoats.

> * Found it while I was doing my big pre-Christmas clean.
> It's at the end of this notebook.

[Two press cuttings about the execution of Quisling, one unidentified, one from Expressen, *24 October 1945.]*

My cuttings don't say enough about the dreadful hardship in Germany. In Vienna and Berlin they reckon all the babies could die this winter.

Coffee came off ration on 1 November (to the delight of all coffee-lovers), along with tea and cocoa. We see the occasional banana now. Tobacco rationing is over, and spices are off ration, too.

And I won first prize for *Pippi Longstocking*, which is coming out any day now. Meanwhile, Sture had to go to London, but didn't like it at all. It was in a sorry state after the war, not much food and so on, dirty and dismal.

Karin's in her first year at the school at Sveaplan and acquitting herself well, ambitious little soul. Lasse's in his final year at upper secondary (after resitting three subjects), we'll see how it goes!

I'm working part-time for the 1944 State Part-Time Work Commission and I sometimes miss the old censor's office. We had a party here on the 13th for my old workmates from Sections 11 and 12 – and I very much wonder whether we'll all meet up like that again.

I just heard a live transmission from Nuremberg. I heard all those butchers stand there and declare themselves *nicht schuldig* [not guilty]. Frank – the butcher of Poland, Streicher, persecutor of Jews, Göring, Hess, the whole lot were as innocent as lambs and assured the court of the fact in steady voices.

25 NOVEMBER

Right now everybody's talking about, and opposing and despairing over, the Swedish government's decision to agree to Russian demands that we hand over large numbers of Baltic refugees, who the Russians want back home so they can kill them. It feels as dishonourable as when we gave way to Germany and let the leave trains pass through Sweden. There are protests from many quarters – I suppose the next few days will prove whether we are really going through with this outrage. How stupid of the Russians to make such a proposal! It only drags into broad daylight the fact that everyone with any experience of Russia knows them to be guilty of atrocities to match any ever committed by the Germans – though it isn't considered opportune to mention it nowadays. They've enough people at home to kill already, without importing any from Sweden.

Shoes and fabrics are coming off ration on Monday, and petrol rationing ends today.

And yesterday I went into a bookshop and bought myself a copy of *Pippi Longstocking*, that jolly funny book, which would never have existed if it weren't for my sprained foot at the end of winter 1944. Not that it would really have mattered, of course!

CHRISTMAS DAY

The snow is falling outside our window and a quiet calm prevails inside, except when Grandmother launches into one of her detailed accounts of events in the lives of people I don't know.

We had a really nice Christmas Eve, peaceful and happy. It feels rather different to last year – I didn't weep into the herring salad. Nor did I have to wear myself out; my part-time job leaves me plenty of time, so I had everything ready well in advance.

Karin was in seventh heaven on Christmas Eve and is just as pleased today. Sture and I thought of going out to Djurgården yesterday but we found ourselves waiting so long for the number 14 that we did a little circuit round Karlbergsvägen and Sankt Eriksplan instead. It's been snowing all day and looks as Christmassy as anything. Yesterday evening there were Christmas carols on the radio and listening to them for a while gave me a sense of utter joy. I feel so undeservedly rich, things are all going well, I have so many friends, I have my home, my children, my Sture, I have virtually everything.

This is the first peacetime Christmas – though here in Sweden the contrast isn't all that marked, seeing as we've been living in the lap of luxury throughout. Unfortunately I don't suppose the change is that noticeable abroad either, there's such terrible, acute need. As I look about me at our warm and cosy home, which looks so nice (if I say so myself) with its white hyacinths and candles and Christmas tree and the pyramid cake on the table, I think about all the pitiful wretches around the world and all the poor children who won't even notice it's Christmas.

My own received the following presents: Lasse a ski jacket, the promise of a ski cap, a story collection called *From the Seven Seas*, gloves, (both my books), a safety razor, marzipan, a shaving brush from Karin, soap from the Lindström cousins, money from Granny and Grandad and Auntie Anna, plus some money from me for a week in Storlien [skiing]. Camel [cigarettes] from Linnéa. Karin had lots of books: [Eric Linklater's] *The Wind on the Moon*, [Erik Lundegård's] *Noses Like Question Marks*, [Lucy Fitch Perkins's] *The Dutch Twins*, a propelling pencil, a sewing box, a toothbrush, a set of undies, marzipan, plus a gorgeous bracelet from Anne-Marie, the high point of the evening, money from Granny and Grandad and Auntie Anna, *Mary Poppins* and *Trekanten* [*The Triangle*, by Inger Bentzon] from Alli and Matte, a painted wooden Dala horse from Britt-Marie Lomm, sewing things from Linnéa, I think that's all, but it's plenty.

Tomorrow the Lindströms are coming for dinner. We'll be having roast reindeer and fruit salad. Today we're having black grouse. Any time now!

I ought to give a list of my presents, too. Sture had been out shopping with the Hedners and the result was a splendid pair of gloves, a twin set I expect I'll take back and change, some galoshes I shall change as well. Two pairs finest silk stockings. I had a fountain pen from Lasse, the one I'm writing with, he bought it second-hand, and a powder puff and some eau de cologne from Karin.

Sture got *ÖÄ's Caricature Album* [collection of classic comic drawings by Oskar Andersson], Hasse Z[etterström]'s *Funny Company*, [Frans G. Bengtsson's] *The Long Ships*, a pile of coat hangers, half a litre of cognac and various bits and bobs from the children, that's to say, *The Long Ships* was from Lasse, and Karin and Lasse gave him a subscription to [the Swedish] *Reader's Digest* – and that's all I can remember.

Pippi is a great little kid who seems to be turning into quite a success. She's been sold to Norway, too. As have *Britt-Mari* and *Kerstin and I*.

So another New Year is almost upon us! They come round so quickly.

Nineteen forty-five brought two remarkable things. Peace after the Second World War and the atom bomb. I wonder what the future will have to say about the atom bomb, and whether it will mark a whole new era in human existence, or not. The peace is not much to put one's faith in, with the atom bomb casting such a shadow over it. They held a conference in Moscow and the papers claim the prospects for world peace are more hopeful as a result, but I shall take that with a pinch of salt. There's desperate hardship in Germany, and people are short of food everywhere except here.

The day after tomorrow I'm going to Småland, joining Karin who's already there. Lasse set off on his trip to Storlien yesterday evening. Sture and I are spending New Year together, accompanied by Grandmother, who returns to her solitary existence in Furusund on Friday, the old stick. Tomorrow Sture and I are going for dinner at the Strand and then to the revue premiere at the Söder [theatre] – it was very different last year. As long as I can keep calm, everything will be fine.

My 'literary' star has been on the rise this year and will no doubt wane in the coming months. *Pippi* got an amazingly enthusiastic reception from the critics, and the public, too, it seems. The verdict on *Kerstin and I* was more mixed, but I'm pretty happy with it all the same and Jeanna Oterdahl wrote that teenagers would like it a lot, and in fact I agree with her, because that sort of slanginess appeals to them. [My play] 'If You Have Your Health and Strength' got a bit of attention, but quite undeservedly because it's not worth wasting words on.

I'm looking ahead to 1946 with excitement and apprehension – for various reasons. Nineteen forty-five has been a very difficult year in parts, especially the first half, but the autumn, too. My job at the censor's office came to an end this year when peace broke out. Since 10 September I've been a shorthand typist at the 1944 State Part-Time Work Commission.

Karin's completed her first term at Norrmalm Girls' Grammar [at Sveaplan] and is getting on well. Lars flunked his English but got Ba [a satisfactory pass] in chemistry and one other subject, which is really good going for him. He's got lots of friends and acquaintances – of both sexes – and is out a lot. Sture, on the other hand, is at home a lot.

All the best for the New Year to me! To me and mine! And ideally to the whole world as well, though that's probably asking too much. But even if it can't be the *best* New Year, perhaps at least it can be a *better* one.

[Press cutting from Dagens Nyheter, 21 August 1945: long article
by Barbro Alving about the start of Quisling's trial in Oslo.]

Stockholm den 27 april 1944.

Albert Bonniers Förlags A/B,
Sveavägen 54-58,
Stockholm.

       Inneliggande tillåter jag mig översända ett barn-
boksmanuskript, som jag med full förtröstan emotser i retur
snarast möjligt.

       Pippi Långstrump är, som Ni kommer att finna, om
Ni gör Er besvär att läsa manuset, en liten Uebermensch i ett
barns gestalt, inflyttad i en helt vanlig miljö. Tack vare sina
övernaturliga kroppskrafter och andra omständigheter är hon helt
oberoende av alla vuxna och lever sitt liv ackurat som det
roar henne. I sina sammandrabbningar med stora människor behåller
hon alltid sista ordet.

       Hos Bertrand Russell (Uppfostran för livet, sid.85)
läser jag, att det förnämsta instinktiva draget i barndomen
är begäret att bli vuxen eller kanske rättare viljan till makt,
och att det normala barnet i fantasien hänger sig åt föreställ-
ningar, som innebära vilja till makt.

       Jag vet inte, om Bertrand Russell har rätt, men
jag är böjd för att tro det, att döma av den rent sjukliga
popularitet, som Pippi Långstrump under en följd av år åtnjutit
hos mina egna barn och deras jämnåriga vänner. Nu är jag natur-
ligtvis inte så förmäten, att jag inbillar mig, att därför att
ett antal barn älskat att höra berättas om Pippis bedrifter,
det nödvändigtvis behöver bli en tryck- och läsbar bok, när
jag skriver ned det på papperet.

       För att övertyga mig om hur det förhåller sig med
den saken, överlämnar jag härmed manuskriptet i Edra sakkunniga
händer och kan bara hoppas, att Ni inte alarmerar barnavårds-
nämnden. För säkerhets skull kanske jag bör påpeka, att mina egna
otroligt väluppfostrade små gussänglar till barn inte rönt
något skadligt inflytande av Pippis uppförande. De ha utan
vidare förstått, att Pippi är en särling, som ingalunda kan
utgöra något mönster för vanliga barn.

              Högaktningsfullt

Fru Astrid Lindgren,
Dalagatan 46, I
Stockholm.

The letter Astrid sent to Bonniers along with her manuscript
of Pippi Longstocking *on 27 April 1944.*

Bonniers

BOK- och TIDSKRIFTSFÖRLAG
FIRMAN GRUNDADES I
KÖPENHAMN   GÖTEBORG   STOCKHOLM
1804   1827   2 7
Gerhard Bonnier   Adolf B.   Albert Bonnier

STOCKHOLM den 20 september 1944.

K.P.

Fru Astrid Lindgren,
Dalagatan 46, I,
STOCKHOLM

       Vi ber om ursäkt för det osedvanligt långa dröjsmålet
med vårt svar. Det har berott på att vi gärna skulle ha velat ge
ut Er bok och manuskriptet har därför fått vandra runt inom för-
laget för läsning, vi har försökt ändra på våra planer så att Ert
manuskript skulle kunna passas in, men tyvärr förgäves. När vi i
förra veckan gick igenom vårt barnboksprogram, visade det sig att
det för Bonniers Barnbiblioteks del finns manuskript inköpta för
hela 1945 och 1946 års produktion och att redan nu binda oss för
1947, det vill vi inte.

       Manuskriptet är mycket orginellt och underhållande i
all sin otrolighet och vi beklagar verkligen att vi inte skall
kunna åtaga oss utgivandet. Vi återsänder det samtidigt med detta
brev som assurerat postpaket.

                         Med utmärkt högaktning

                       ALBERT BONNIERS FÖRLAG A.B.

*Bonnier's famous letter of 20 September 1944, rejecting
the manuscript of Pippi Longstocking.*

Glossary of Names

Abrahamsson (Mr and Mrs), friends of Alice and Per Viridén, through whom they knew Astrid and Sture Lindgren

Adin (Mrs), teacher of Astrid Lindgren's daughter Karin

Agapit, Jean-Jacques, French writer

Alli, see Viridén, Alice

Alvtegen, Barbro (1937–), Astrid Lindgren's niece, her brother's daughter

Anders, see Bené, Anders

Anna, see Eriksson, Anna

Anne-Marie, see Fries, Anne-Marie

Astrid (1905–35), Swedish princess who married Crown Prince Leopold of Belgium in 1926, queen of the Belgians 1934–35

Attlee, Clement (1883–1967), British prime minister 1945–51

Badoglio, Pietro (1871–1956), Italian politician and general, prime minister 1943–44

Bågstam, Tage (1917–2004), illustrator, presumably one of Astrid Lindgren's colleagues at the censor's office

Barbro, see Alvtegen, Barbro

Beckman, presumably a journalist at the Swedish news agency TT (Tidningarnas Telegrambyrå)

Bedell Smith, Walter (1895–1961), American army officer and diplomat, Eisenhower's chief-of-staff, US ambassador to the Soviet Union 1946–48

Bené, Anders, son of Karin Bené

Bené, Karin, one of the young mothers who used to meet in Vasa Park

Berggrav, Eivind (1884–1959), Norwegian bishop and theologian, opponent of Quisling, kept under house arrest 1942–45

Bernadotte, Folke (1895–1948), Swedish officer and diplomat

Böök, Fredrik (1883–1961), Swedish literary historian and critic

Boris III of Bulgaria (1894–1943), tsar of Bulgaria 1918–43

Brauchitsch, Walther von (1881–1948), supreme commander of the German army 1938–41

Brunius, Célie (1882–1980), Swedish journalist

Capra, Frank (1897–1991), Italian-American film director

Carol II of Romania (1893–1953), king of Romania 1930–40

Chamberlain, Neville (1869–1940), prime minister of Great Britain 1937–40

Christian X of Denmark (1870–1947), king of Denmark 1912–47

Churchill, Winston (1874–1965), prime minister of Great Britain 1940–45 and 1951–55, awarded the Nobel Prize in Literature 1953

Ciano, Edda (1910–95), daughter of Benito Mussolini, married Galeazzo Ciano 1930

Ciano, Galeazzo (1903–44), Italian politician and diplomat, foreign minister 1936–43

Clausen, Frits (1893–1947), leader of the National Socialist Workers' Party of Denmark 1933–44

Dad, see Ericsson, Samuel August

Darlan, François (1881–1942), French admiral and politician, minister for the navy and the merchant fleet in the Vichy regime 1940–41, deputy prime minister, foreign minister and minister of the interior 1941–42

De Gaulle, Charles (1890–1970), brigadier-general and leader of the Free France Forces 1940–44, head of the provisional government of the French Republic 1940–46 and president 1959–69

De la Gardie, Pontus (1884–1970), Swedish count

de Mumma, Kar, see Kar de Mumma

Dieden, Elsebeth ('Pelle') (1906–95), friend of the Lindgren family

Diktonius, Elmer (1896–1961), Finland-Swedish writer, composer and critic

Dönitz, Karl (1891–1980), German naval commander

Dubois, Nils (1900–71), colleague of Astrid Lindgren at the censor's office

Eden, Anthony (1897–1977), British foreign minister 1935–38, 1940–45 and 1951–55, prime minister 1955–57

Eisenhower, Dwight D. (1890–1969), Supreme Allied Commander in Western Europe during the Second World War, US president 1953–1961

Elsa, see Gullander, Elsa

Elsa-Lena, see Oliv, Elsa-Lena

Emil, no information available

Engberg, Arthur (1888–1944), Swedish Social Democrat politician, minister of ecclesiastical affairs 1932–36 and 1936–39

Engström, Albert (1869–1940), Swedish writer and artist

Ericsson, Gunnar (1906–74), Astrid Lindgren's brother, national representative of the Swedish Rural Youth League 1936–42 and Centre Party member of parliament in the Second Chamber 1946–56

Ericsson, Hanna (also referred to as Granny, Mum) (1879–1961), née Jonsson, Astrid Lindgren's mother

Ericsson, Samuel August (also referred to as Grandad, Dad) (1875–1969), Astrid Lindgren's father

Eriksson, Anna (1889–1986), Astrid Lindgren's aunt, her father's sister

Eriksson, Tekla ('Lecka'), sister-in-law of Gun Eriksson with whom Astrid Lindgren lived when she first moved to Stockholm

Esse, see Stevens, John

Eveo, see Olson, Erik Vilhelm

Fåhreus, no information available

Falk, Britta-Kajsa, friend of Lars Lindgren

Fangen, Ronald (1895–1946), Norwegian writer, journalist and critic

Father, see Lindgren, Nils

Flory, see Shanke, Florence

Franco, Francisco (1892–1975), Spain's head of state and dictator 1939–75

Frank, Hans (1900–46), German Nazi politician, executed at Nuremberg

Fries, Anne-Marie (1907–91), Astrid Lindgren's best friend from the time of their childhood, who worked with Astrid at the censor's office

Fries, Stellan (1902–93), husband of Anne-Marie Fries

Gandhi, Mohandas Karamchand, known as Mahatma (1869–1948), leader of the Indian National Congress, who advocated non-violent non-cooperation to achieve independence

Gerhard, Karl (1891–1964), Swedish theatre director, actor and revue writer who opposed Nazism. During the Second World War he staged revues critical of Germany.

Gierow, Karl Ragnar (1904–82), Swedish director and writer, permanent secretary of the Swedish Academy 1964–77

Goebbels, Joseph (1897–1945) German minister of propaganda 1933–45

Göran, see Stäckig, Göran

Göring, Hermann (1893–1946), speaker of the German parliament, founder of the Gestapo, commander of the Luftwaffe 1935–45

Grandmother, see Lindgren, Karolina

Grandad, see Ericsson, Samuel August

Granny, see Ericsson, Hanna

Grieg, Nordahl (1902–43), Norwegian writer, journalist and freedom fighter

Grimberg, Carl (1875–1941), Swedish historian and publisher

Gullander, Elsa (1900–97), one of the young mothers who used to meet in Vasa Park

Gullander, Nils Emil Sigurd ('Sigge') (1884–1971), married to Elsa Gullander

Gunnar, see Ericsson, Gunnar

Günther, Christian (1886–1966), Swedish foreign minister 1939–45

Gunvor, see Runström, Gunvor

Gustaf V (1858–1950), king of Sweden 1907–50

Haakon VII of Norway (1872–1957), king of Norway 1905–57

Hägg, Gunder (1918–2004), Swedish middle-distance runner

Håkansson, Hans, see Hergin, Hans

Hamberg, Per-Martin (1912–74), colleague of Astrid Lindgren at the censor's office, and a close friend

Hanna, see Ericsson, Hanna

Hans, see Hergin, Hans

Hansson, Per Albin (1885–1946), party chairman the Swedish Social Democratic Party 1925–46 and Swedish prime minister 1932–46, apart from three months in 1936

Hansteen, Viggo (1900–41), Norwegian lawyer and Communist politician, executed by the Quisling regime

Harrie, Ivar (1899–1973), Swedish journalist, editor in chief of *Expressen* 1944–60

Hedner, Brita, wife of Carl-Erik Hedner

Hedner, Carl-Erik, lawyer at the Swedish motorists' association Motormännens Riksförbund and a close colleague of Sture Lindgren. The Hedners and the Lindgrens also met socially.

Hedner, Gunnel, second wife of Carl-Erik Hedner

Heidenstam, Verner von (1859–1940), Swedish writer and poet, awarded the Nobel Prize in Literature in 1916

Helbig, Inger (1940–), née Lindström, Astrid Lindgren's niece, her sister Ingegerd's daughter

Helena of Greece (1896–1982), first wife of Carol II of Romania and mother of Michael I of Romania

Hemmer, Jarl (1893–1944), Finland-Swedish writer

Hergin, Hans (1910–88), born Håkansson, Swedish proletarian writer, married to Astrid Lindgren's sister Stina

Hergin, Stina (1911–02), née Ericsson, Astrid Lindgren's sister

Hess, Rudolf (1894–87), German Nazi politician, deputy Führer 1933–41, captured in Scotland during an abortive attempt to broker peace with Britain

Heydrich, Reinhard (1904–42), chief of the Reich security head office, deputy protector of Bohemia and Moravia, one of the main architects of the Holocaust, assassinated in Prague

Himmler, Heinrich (1900–45), head of the SS 1929–45

Hitler, Adolf (1889–1945), chairman of the Nazi Party, Chancellor of Germany 1933–45 and dictator 1939–45

Hull, Cordell (1871–1955), American Democrat politician, US secretary of state 1933–44

Hultstrand (Mr and Mrs), probably friends of Alice and Per Viridén, no further information available

Ingegerd, see Lindström, Ingegerd

Ingman, Brita, married to Nils Ingman, the two of them part of Astrid and Sture Lindgren's social circle via their acquaintance with the Viridéns

Ingman, Nils, married to Brita Ingman

Ingrid from Brofall, married to Astrid Lindgren's cousin Erik from Åbro

Ingvar, see Lindström, Ingvar

Ingvarsdotter, Inger, see Helbig, Inger

Jerring, Sven (1895–1979), born Jonsson, Swedish radio presenter

Jodl, Alfred (1890–1946), German general, signed Germany's unconditional surrender on all fronts in 1945

Johansson, Gerd (1929–39), young Swedish girl who was murdered

Johnson, Eyvind (1900–76), Swedish writer, awarded the Nobel Prize in Literature in 1974

Juliana, princess of the Netherlands (1909–2004), queen 1948–80, crown princess throughout the Second World War

Kallio, Kyösti (1873–1940), president of Finland 1937–40

Kar de Mumma (1904–97), pseudonym of Erik Zetterström, Swedish revue writer and columnist

Karin, see Nyman, Karin

Karlsson, Gustav Adolf (1884–1960), Swedish clairvoyant

Karlsson, Karin, daughter of Johan Karlsson the cowman at Näs, where Astrid Lindgren grew up, and the same age as Astrid Lindgren's daughter Karin

Kivimäki, Toivo Mikael (1886–1968), Finnish prime minister 1932–36, ambassador to Germany 1940–44

Kjellberg, Lennart (1913–2004), colleague of Astrid Lindgren at the censor's office

Kock, officer, no further information available

Kurusu, Saburō (1886–1954), Japan's ambassador to Germany 1939–41, later sent to the USA to conduct peace negotiations and interned after the attack on Pearl Harbor in 1941

Kuusinen, Otto Wille (1881–1964), head of the Soviet Union's puppet government in Finland 1939–40

Lagerblad, Ragnar and Ingerborg, acquaintances of the Lindgrens. Ragnar was in the printing business.

Lagerkvist, Pär (1891–1974), Swedish writer, awarded the Nobel Prize in Literature in 1951

Lagerlöf, Selma (1858–1940), Swedish writer, awarded the Nobel Prize in Literature in 1909

Lasse, see Lindgren, Lars

Laval, Pierre (1883–1945), French politician, member of the Vichy regime and its prime minister 1942–44

Leander, Zarah (1907–81), Swedish singer and actress, one of the biggest film stars in Germany during the Second World War

Lecka, see Eriksson, Tekla

Leopold III (1901–83), king of the Belgians 1934–51

Lindgren, Karolina (also referred to as Mother and Grandmother) (1865–1947), Sture Lindgren's mother

Lindgren, Lars ('Lasse') (1926–86), Astrid Lindgren's son

Lindgren, Nils (also referred to as Father) (1868–1940), Sture Lindgren's father

Lindgren, Sture (1898–1952), Astrid Lindgren's husband, managing director of the Swedish motorists' association Motormännens Riksförbund 1941–52

Lindner, Karl Gunnar (1901–43), Swedish aircraft pilot

Lindström, Åke (1944–68), Astrid Lindgren's nephew, son of Ingegerd Lindström

Lindström, Ingegerd (1916–97), née Ericsson, Astrid Lindgren's sister

Lindström, Ingvar (1911–87), married to Astrid Lindgren's sister Ingegerd

Linkomies, Edwin (1894–1963), prime minister of Finland 1943–44

Linnéa, see Molander, Linnéa

Litiäinen, Karin, one of the young mothers who used to meet in Vasa Park

Litvinov, Maxim (1876–1951), Soviet politician and diplomat, ambassador to the USA 1941–43

Lomm, Britt-Marie (1932–), granddaughter of Astrid Lindgren's neighbour at their summer cottage at Furusund

Lövenskiöld Lövenborg, Carl Oscar Herman Leopold, Norwegian count

Lupescu, Magda (1895–1977), married Carol II of Romania in 1947

Mannerheim, Carl Gustaf (1867–1951), supreme commander of the Finnish army 1939–46 and president of Finland 1944–1946

Marie José of Belgium (1906–2001), married Umberto II of Italy, queen of Italy briefly in 1946

Märtha of Norway (1901–54), crown princess of Norway and princess of Sweden, married Olav V of Norway in 1929

Matte, see Viridén, Margareta

Maugham, W. Somerset (1874–1965), British writer

Maurois, André (1885–1967), French writer

Medin, Elisabeth, mother of Florence Shanke who was a colleague of Astrid Lindgren at the censor's office

Michael I of Romania (1921–), king of Romania 1927–30 and 1940–47

Mistral, Gabriela (1889–1957), pseudonym of Lucila Godoy y Alcayaga, Chilean poet and educator, awarded the Nobel Prize in Literature in 1945

Molander, Linnéa, home help to the Lindgren family 1939–50

Molin, Aina, no information available

Möller, Olle (1906–1983), Swedish sportsman and potato seller who was convicted of two notorious murders, despite his denial of the charges

Molotov, Vyacheslav (1890–1986), foreign minister of the Soviet Union 1939–49 and 1953–56

Mörne, Håkan (1900–1961), Finland-Swedish writer

Mother, see Lindgren, Karolina

Mum, see Ericsson, Hanna

Munk, Kaj (1898–1944), Danish dramatist and clergyman, murdered by the Gestapo

Mussolini, Benito (1883–1945), Fascist dictator of Italy 1922–43

Nilsson, Rut, probably a colleague of Astrid Lindgren at the censor's office

Nirsch, presumably a colleague of Astrid Lindgren at the censor's office, no further information available

Norwid, Stefan Tadeusz (1902–76), pseudonym of Polish writer Tadeusz Nowacki

Nyberg, (Miss), presumably friend of Alice and Per Viridén, no further information available

Nygaardsvold, Johan (1879–1952), Norwegian Social Democrat politician, prime minister 1935–45, led the government in exile from London, 1940–45

Nygren, (Miss), no information available

Nyman, Karin (1934–), née Lindgren, Astrid Lindgren's daughter

Olav V of Norway (1903–91), king of Norway 1957–91, crown prince during the Second World War

Oliv, Elsa-Lena (1934–), née Gullander, childhood friend of Astrid's daughter Karin, Elsa Gullander's daughter

Olson, Erik Vilhelm ('Eveo') (1891–1970), Swedish writer, journalist and director

Oterdahl, Jeanna (1879–1965), Swedish writer and teacher

Ottander, doctor who treated Astrid Lindgren's daughter Karin, no
    further information available

Øverland, Arnulf (1889–1968), Norwegian writer and lyric poet

Paasikivi, Juho Kusti (1870–1956), Finnish politician and diplomat,
    ambassador to Sweden 1936–40, to Moscow 1940–41, prime minister
    1944–46, president 1946–56

Palmgren (Mr and Mrs), presumably friends of Alice and Per Viridén
    and acquainted with the Lindgrens through them, no further infor-
    mation available

Paul of Yugoslavia (1893–1976), cousin of Peter II, ruled as regent
    1934–1941, until Peter was declared of age

Per-Martin, see Hamberg, Per-Martin

Pétain, Philippe (1856–1951), French head of state 1940–44 under the
    Vichy regime

Peter, see Viridén, Peter

Peter II of Yugoslavia (1923–1970), king of Yugoslavia 1934–45

Quisling, Vidkun (1887–1945), Norwegian politician and founder of
    the fascist Nasjonal Samling (National Unity Party), Norwegian
    minister president 1942–45 under German occupation

Remarque, Erich Maria (1898–1970), German writer

Reynaud, Paul (1878–1966), French politician, president of the Council
    of Ministers for three months in 1940

Ribbentrop, Joachim von (1893–1946), German foreign minister
    1938–45

Rommel, Erwin (1891–1944), army general, commander of Germany's
    Afrika Korps

Roosevelt, Franklin D. (1882–1945), US president 1933–45

Rosén, no information available

Rudling, Arvid (1899–1984), lawyer in whose office Astrid Lindgren worked as a shorthand typist

Runström, Gunvor (1934–), née Ericsson, Astrid Lindgren's niece, her brother's daughter

Rut, see Nilsson, Rut

Rydick, presumably a colleague of Astrid Lindgren at the censor's office, no further information available

Ryti, Risto (1889–1956), president of Finland 1940–44

Samuel August, see Ericsson, Samuel August

Sandemose, Aksel (1899–1965), Danish-Norwegian writer

Sandler, Rickard (1884–1964), Swedish Social Democrat politician, prime minister 1925–26 and foreign minister 1932–36 and 1936–39

Segerfelt, childhood friend of Astrid Lindgren's son Lars, no further information available

Selassie I, Haile (1892–1975), emperor of Ethiopia 1930–74

Shanke, Florence ('Flory') (1918–), née Medin, colleague of Astrid Lindgren at the censor's office

Sibylla of Saxe-Coburg-Gotha (1908–72), Swedish princess, wife of hereditary prince Gustaf Adolf

Sigge, see Gullander, Nils Emil Sigurd

Sillanpää, Frans Eemil (1888–1964), Finnish writer, awarded the Nobel Prize in Literature 1939

Silfverstolpe, Gunnar Mascoll (1893–1942), Swedish poet, translator and critic

Simeon II (1937–), king of Bulgaria 1943–46

Skyllerstedt, presumably a colleague of Astrid Lindgren at the censor's office, no further information available

Stäckig, Göran (1926–2007), childhood friend of Lars Lindgren

Stäckig, Signe Elisabeth (1899–1974), née Lundström, mother of Göran
Stäckig

Stalin, Joseph (1878–1953), secretary general of the Communist Party
of the Soviet Union 1922–52, after the death of Lenin in practice
assumed power over the country as a dictator, also formally head
of government from 1941

Stauning, Thorvald (1873–1942), Danish Social Democrat politician,
prime minister 1924–26 and 1929–42

Stellan, see Fries, Stellan

Stevens, John ('Esse') (1925–2007), Lars Lindgren's foster brother for the
first three years of Lars's life, when he was cared for by the Stevens
family in Copenhagen

Stina, see Hergin, Stina

Stolpe, Sven (1905–96), Swedish writer, journalist and literary critic

Streicher, Julius (1885–1946), German Nazi politician

Strindlund, Gerhard (1890–1957), Swedish politician, member of
Bondeförbundet (the Farmers' League), minister of social affairs
1936 and communication minister 1938–39

Sture, see Lindgren, Sture

Svensson, Johan Petter ('Lucke'), 'Vimmerby's toughest old boy',
according to the local paper *Vimmerby Tidning*

Taina, presumably an evacuated Finnish war child, staying with Elsa
Gullander

Tanner, Väinö (1881–1966), Finnish Social Democrat politician, finance
minister 1937–1939, foreign minister 1939–40 and minister for trade
and industry 1940–42

Tedder, Arthur (1890–1967), senior British air force commander

Terboven, Josef (1898–1945), German Nazi politician, Reichskommissar
for Norway during its occupation 1940–45

Tjerneld, Staffan (1910–89), Swedish journalist and writer

Truman, Harry S. (1884–1972), American Democratic politician, US vice president 1945 and, following the death of Franklin D. Roosevelt, president 1945–53

Umberto II of Italy (1904–1983), king of Italy briefly in 1946

Victor Emmanuel III (1869–1947), king of Italy 1900–46

Viridén, Alice ('Alli') (1904–2003), close friend of Astrid Lindgren and one of the young mothers who used to meet in Vasa Park

Viridén, Margareta ('Matte') (1934–), childhood friend of Astrid's daughter Karin and daughter of Alice Viridén

Viridén, Per ('Pelle') (1902-86), married to Alice Viridén

Viridén, Peter, son of Alice Viridén

Virtanen, Rauno, presumably a Finnish acquaintance of Astrid's brother Gunnar Ericsson, who was involved in Swedish aid to Finland

Wendt, Georg von (1876–1954), Finnish medical research scientist and politician

Wenner-Gren, Axel (1881–1961), Swedish business leader and financier

Wickman, Johannes (1882–1957), Swedish publicist, foreign affairs editor of *Dagens Nyheter* 1918–48

Wickstrøm, Rolf (1912–1941), Norwegian trade unionist, put to death by the Quisling regime

Wikberg, Greta, no information available

Wilhelm II of Germany (1859–1941), German emperor and king of Prussia 1888–1918 and subsequently lived in the Netherlands

Wilhelmina of the Netherlands (1880–1962), queen of the Netherlands 1890–1948

Willkie, Wendell (1892–1944), American Republican politician, presidential candidate and challenger of Franklin D. Roosevelt in the 1940 election

Wrede af Elimä, Brita Anna (1894–1973), writer and film producer

Wuolijoki, Hella (1886–1954), Estonian-born Finnish writer

Wuori, Eero (1900–66), Finnish Social Democrat politician and cabinet minister

Zetterström, Erik (1904–97), Swedish comic writer and columnist who sometimes wrote under the pseudonym Kar de Mumma

Zweig, Stefan (1881–1942), Austrian writer

Pushkin Press

Pushkin Press was founded in 1997, and publishes novels, essays, memoirs, children's books—everything from timeless classics to the urgent and contemporary.

Our books represent exciting, high-quality writing from around the world: we publish some of the twentieth century's most widely acclaimed, brilliant authors such as Stefan Zweig, Marcel Aymé, Teffi, Antal Szerb, Gaito Gazdanov and Yasushi Inoue, as well as compelling and award-winning contemporary writers, including Andrés Neuman, Edith Pearlman, Eka Kurniawan and Ayelet Gundar-Goshen.

Pushkin Press publishes the world's best stories, to be read and read again. Here are just some of the titles from our long and varied list. To discover more, visit www.pushkinpress.com.

═══

THE SPECTRE OF ALEXANDER WOLF
GAITO GAZDANOV

'A mesmerising work of literature' Antony Beevor

SUMMER BEFORE THE DARK
VOLKER WEIDERMANN

'For such a slim book to convey with such poignancy the extinction of a generation of "Great Europeans" is a triumph' *Sunday Telegraph*

MESSAGES FROM A LOST WORLD
STEFAN ZWEIG

'At a time of monetary crisis and political disorder... Zweig's celebration of the brotherhood of peoples reminds us that there is another way' *The Nation*

BINOCULAR VISION
EDITH PEARLMAN

'A genius of the short story' Mark Lawson, *Guardian*

IN THE BEGINNING WAS THE SEA
TOMÁS GONZÁLEZ

'Smoothly intriguing narrative, with its touches of sinister, Patricia Highsmith-like menace' *Irish Times*

BEWARE OF PITY
STEFAN ZWEIG

'Zweig's fictional masterpiece' *Guardian*

THE ENCOUNTER
PETRU POPESCU

'A book that suggests new ways of looking at the world and our place within it' *Sunday Telegraph*

WAKE UP, SIR!
JONATHAN AMES

'The novel is extremely funny but it is also sad and poignant, and almost incredibly clever' *Guardian*

THE WORLD OF YESTERDAY
STEFAN ZWEIG

'*The World of Yesterday* is one of the greatest memoirs of the twentieth century, as perfect in its evocation of the world Zweig loved, as it is in its portrayal of how that world was destroyed' David Hare

WAKING LIONS
AYELET GUNDAR-GOSHEN

'A literary thriller that is used as a vehicle to explore big moral issues. I loved everything about it' *Daily Mail*

BONITA AVENUE
PETER BUWALDA

'One wild ride: a swirling helix of a family saga… a new writer as toe-curling as early Roth, as roomy as Franzen and as caustic as Houellebecq' *Sunday Telegraph*

JOURNEY BY MOONLIGHT
ANTAL SZERB

'Just divine… makes you imagine the author has had private access to your own soul' Nicholas Lezard, *Guardian*

THE RABBIT BACK LITERATURE SOCIETY
PASI ILMARI JÄÄSKELÄINEN

'Wonderfully knotty… a very grown-up fantasy masquerading as quirky fable. Unexpected, thrilling and absurd' *Sunday Telegraph*

STAMMERED SONGBOOK: A MOTHER'S BOOK OF HOURS
ERWIN MORTIER

'Mortier has a poet's eye for vibrant detail and prose to match… If this is a book of fragmentation, it is also a son's moving tribute' *Observer*

BARCELONA SHADOWS
MARC PASTOR

'As gruesome as it is gripping… the writing is extraordinarily vivid… Highly recommended' *Independent*

THE LIBRARIAN
MIKHAIL ELIZAROV

'A romping good tale… Pretty sensational' *Big Issue*

WHILE THE GODS WERE SLEEPING
ERWIN MORTIER

'A monumental, phenomenal book' *De Morgen*

BUTTERFLIES IN NOVEMBER
AUÐUR AVA ÓLAFSDÓTTIR

'A funny, moving and occasionally bizarre exploration of life's upheavals and reversals' *Financial Times*

BY BLOOD
ELLEN ULLMAN

'Delicious and intriguing' *Daily Telegraph*

THE LAST DAYS
LAURENT SEKSIK

'Mesmerising… Seksik's portrait of Zweig's final months is dignified and tender' *Financial Times*

TALKING TO OURSELVES
ANDRÉS NEUMAN

'This is writing of a quality rarely encountered… when you read Neuman's beautiful novel, you realise a very high bar has been set' *Guardian*